LUNDY — ISLAND WITHOUT EQUAL

LUNDY
Island without Equal

by Lois Lamplugh

Robert Young

Published by Robert Young, Bookseller and Publisher,
Swimbridge, near Barnstaple, Devon

© Lois Lamplugh 1993

British Library Cataloguing-in-Publication Data:
A CIP catalogue record for this book is available from
the British Library.

ISBN 1 898360 01 4

Typesetting by Dennis C. Hain, Barnstaple, Devon.
Printed by Printing Matters (Bude) Limited,
Bude, Cornwall.

All rights reserved. No part of this publication may
be reproduced, stored in a retrieval system, or
transmitted in any form or by any means, electronic,
mechanical, photocopying, recording or otherwise
without the prior permission of the copyright holder.

CONTENTS

List of Text Illustrations	ii
List of Plates	iii
Acknowledgements and Note on the Lundy of today under the administration of the Landmark Trust	iv
Chapter	
1	1
2	7
3	13
4	23
5	32
6	40
7	48
8	55
9	68
10	77
11	87
12	96
13	108
14	118
15	129
Notes	142
Bibliography	147
Index	148

List of Text Illustrations

	Page
Head of a puffin, issued as a half-puffin stamp	1
Diamond-shaped stamp showing the Knight Templar Rock. Half-puffin value. 1962. (Designed by Whiteley)	7
Another diamond-shaped stamp of 1962, showing a peregrine falcon. Two puffin value.	13
Chapter Tail: an 18th century engraving of the Marisco Castle from Grose's ANTIQUITIES	22
A stamp designed by John Dyke showing the Marisco Castle. One puffin value. 1954	23
Chapter Tail: a line drawing of puffins, by John Dyke	31
Another of the 1954 set of stamps designed by John Dyke, showing the Constable Rock. Nine puffin value	32
Stamp showing an 18th century sailing ship, designed to celebrate the bicentenary of the American Declaration of Independence. Twelve puffin value. 1976	40
Chapter Tail: a drawing by Philip Gosse, 'Guillemot and Gannet'	47
A stamp issued in 1972 showing the Old Light, with keepers in Trinity House uniforms. One puffin value	48
One of a set of four stamps issued in 1975 to celebrate European Heritage Year, showing Millcombe House, built in 1836 by William Hudson Heaven. Known to the Heaven family as The Villa, it was renamed Millcombe by Martin Coles Harman. Eight puffin value	55
Chapter Tail: The Mousetrap, by Philip Gosse	67
One of a set of stamps designed by John Dyke to celebrate the 75th anniversary of the consecration of St Helena's Church. One puffin value, 1972	68
A stamp showing stores being landed from the M.V. *Lerina*, Lundy's supply vessel from 1929 - 1950. Eight puffin value	77
Chapter Tail: 'Entrance to the Cavern' by Philip Gosse	86
Stamp designed by John Dyke showing the *Lundy Gannet*. Two puffin value. 1969	87
Chapter Tail: one of the air mail stamps issued by Atlantic Coast Air Services showing an aircraft flying from Barnstaple Aerodrome to Lundy in 1936	95

Another of the stamps issued to celebrate European Heritage Year in
    1975, showing 'The position of Europe in relation to Lundy'
    — a concept that would surely have appealed to Martin Harman
    if it had appeared during his lifetime. Ten puffin value   96
This stamp, showing the mail bag being carried from the airfield towards
    the Marisco Tavern, with an aircraft flying overhead, is one of a set
    celebrating the 50th anniversary of the Lundy post inaugurated by
    Martin Harman. Eleven and a half puffin value. 1979   108
Chapter Tail: a stamp designed by John Dyke showing the postmaster
    Frederick Allday with the donkey allotted to him to carry the mail.
    One puffin value. 1969   117
The nine puffin stamp from the set designed by John Dyke for the 75th
    anniversary of the consecration of St Helena's Church.   118
Chapter Tail: Lundy Ponies, the four puffin stamp from the set issued
    in 1955 to celebrate the millenary of the unification of England
    under one king. Designed by Ilett   128
Stamp celebrating the designation of Lundy as Britain's first Marine
    Nature Reserve. Eleven and a half puffin value. 1978   129

List of Plates

		Between pages:
1.	Devil's Slide	4 and 5
2.	Marisco Castle	26 and 27
3.	The East side of the island, looking north	36 and 37
4.	The Old Light	52 and 53
5.	William Hudson Heaven	60 and 61
6.	Millcombe House	72 and 73
7.	Victorian paddle steamers	80 and 81
8.	Trinity House gunners and their wives at the Battery	90 and 91
9.	Felix Gade on the Landing Beach	100 and 101
10.	The inner bar (formerly Marisco Cottage) of the Marisco Tavern	120 and 121

Acknowledgements

I would like to offer my thanks to the following:

To the Landmark Trust for permission to reproduce the photographs which appear as plates 1, 2, 3, 4, 5, 6, 7, 8 and 10, the stamps which are reproduced at the head of each chapter and at the tails of chapters 11, 13 and 14, and the pictorial map of Lundy by John Dyke.

To Knights Photographers of Barnstaple for permission to reproduce the photograph of Felix Gade which appears as plate 9.

To John Dyke for permission to reproduce the line drawing of puffins on page 31.

To Wendy and John Puddy for reading this book in typescript and offering encouragement.

In addition, without the resources of the North Devon Athenaeum, the North Devon Record Office and Local Studies Centre Libraries, research would have been considerably slower and more difficult. Thanks are due to the helpful staff of all three.

A Note on the Lundy of Today
National Trust / Landmark Trust

When, in 1969, the generosity of Sir Jack Hayward made it possible for the National Trust to consider fulfilling the hopes of many people by buying Lundy, the decision to accept was made easier by an offer from the Landmark Trust to accept responsibility for the administration and maintenance of the island.

The Landmark Trust had been founded only four years earlier, by John (now Sir John) Smith and his wife Christian, with the stated purpose of preserving 'small buildings, structures or sites of historic interest, architechtural merit, or amenity value,' and where possible to find suitable uses for them. Now it set about a programme of restoring Lundy's buildings, from the Marisco Castle to the former Admiralty lookout on Tibbett's Hill, and converting them so that they could bring in much-needed money: the island has to earn its keep. There are now 23 holiday cottages of widely different types and sizes, as well as a small sheltered camp site. It's possible for over a hundred people to stay on the island at any time of the year, crossing from Bideford or Ilfracombe on Lundy's own passenger/supply ship, the M.S. *Oldenburg*.

Chapter One.

Throughout my childhood Lundy was a shape on the western horizon, appearing and disappearing like an island in a legend. It is not surprising that to the Welsh writer of the MABINOGION it was Caer Sidi, the Fairy Fortress. From the hill above my home in the valley that runs down from Georgeham to Croyde, looking out over Woolacombe Bay, it might be seen as a grape-dark, far-off blur; it might stand out, clear and distinct, having apparently moved a dozen miles shoreward overnight. Very occasionally it was, in the words of a much-quoted local weather rhyme, 'Lundy high, sign of dry': so high that it seemed to float in the air, like the island of Aeolus, keeper of the winds, in Book I of the Aeneid. And at other times it would disappear completely, obliterated by rain or sea mist. To me, as a child, it was inaccessible, since no one in my family felt its fascination as I did.

Although during summers of the early Thirties, at school in Ilfracombe, I often saw one of the majestic paddle steamers of the Campbell brothers' White Funnel Fleet sailing along the coast, bound for Lundy with crowded decks, or coming in to land her day's passengers at the pier, I was sixteen before I was able to go on a steamer trip to the island. A friend from London came to spend a week or two in Georgeham. He had spent holidays there before, and each time had meant to visit Lundy, but somehow never managed it. This year he sent for Campbell timetables and made plans. He had no car, and there was no direct bus service from Georgeham to Ilfracombe, but we could walk by way of the Spraecombe Valley to the A361, the main Braunton-Ilfracombe road, and catch a bus there.

In those years the paddle steamers running day trips to Lundy included the *Glen Usk*, the *Waverley*, the *Cambria*, the *Glen Avon*, the *Ravenswood* and several others. When we reached Ilfracombe the *Glen Usk* was in harbour. We leaned on the warm wooden bulwark and looked down at the great black timber stanchions that supported the pier; underwater they joined iron pillars, orange with rust, going down into oily darkness. Because the steamers came alongside the pier bow first, they had to reverse across the outer harbour when leaving, the paddles churning the water to a brilliant foaming green, as though creme de menthe were being stirred with champagne in a vast vat. Once in the open sea the ship's breadth amidships, caused by the paddles in their protective casings, produced a very wide wake.

In the midst of the lower deck, a glass enclosure revealed the cranks of the paddles pulsing up and down, bright and clean as chrome, the sort of display now only seen in working museums of 19th century industry: an impressive illustration of the efficiency of Victorian steam power lingering into the first half of the 20th.

As we sailed westwards a long, dark, apparently almost level bar of rock grew steadily larger. It was a day of sun and high, slow-moving white clouds. True to its reputation as a weather indicator, the island was reassuringly softened by haze, and so not 'Lundy plain, sign of rain'. Looking back, it was fascinating to see, for the first time, the familiar coast in reverse: there were Morte Point, and Woolacombe Bay, and Baggy Point, and Croyde Bay, and the long beaches of Saunton and Westward Ho! divided by the estuary of the rivers Taw and Torridge.

The sea was calm; there was no danger of being unable to land, as sometimes happened in rough weather, when passengers, having endured a choppy crossing, were dismayed to learn that they would not be set ashore.

Gradually the granite cliffs grew clearer; it was possible to make out Rat Island on the south side of the landing beach, and the South Light, built by Trinity House in the late 19th century.

When the anchor splashed down, and we were queuing for the boats that would take us to the beach — since Lundy lacked, and still lacks, a pier at which ships the size of the *Glen Usk* can come alongside — it was announced that we would sail again in four hours' time: a hooter would be sounded to give half an hour's warning. This meant that once at the top of the steep winding track to the village, four hundred feet above sea level, not much more than three hours remained to do — what? Walk to the far north end of the island? It was quite possible: six miles there and back. Yet we were somehow bemused, as perhaps many first-time visitors are, by the mere fact of being on Lundy at last. Like many of our fellow passengers we wandered around the contrasting structures of the south end: the ruined castle for so long wrongly supposed to have been built by the medieval lords of Lundy, the Mariscos; the unused lighthouse on Beacon Hill and the neat white tower of the South Light; St Helena's Church; Millcombe House; the farm buildings; the Marisco Tavern. We ate our packed lunch somewhere near the terrifying Devil's Limekiln and walked to the Quarter Wall, where an ink-black pool fills old quarry workings left by the fortunately short-lived Lundy Granite Company.

When the *Glen Usk's* hooter boomed across the landing bay and echoed along the cliffs, there was a temptation to ignore it and be left on the island until she called again; we had been told that visitors sometimes did this, and were put up at the hotel. Reluctantly we followed other passengers trailing downhill to the beach. Soon everybody was aboard, and Lundy was dwindling astern, resuming its legendary aspect.

The war came, and I left Devon. With the return of peace, I moved to London. As soon as I could, I spent a holiday in north Devon. The Campbell steamers were running again. In the Second World War, they had been requisitioned and some had been lost. The survivors had been joined by a new paddle steamer, the *Bristol Queen*; she was completed just over a year after the war ended by Charles Hill of Bristol. and sailed down the north coasts of Somerset and Devon on her maiden voyage in September, 1946, to be greeted at Ilfracombe with jubilant salvoes of rockets. She has been described as 'the ultimate in paddle steamer design'[1].

In the decades after the Second World War, Lundy was well served by the Campbell steamers — as were Clovelly, Lynmouth, Ilfracombe and a number of places in South Wales. The White

Funnel Fleet's timetables described their vessels — which in those years included not only the *Bristol Queen* and the *Glen Usk* but the *Cardiff Queen, Lundy Queen, St Trillo, Westward Ho!* and *Waverley* — as being approximately 245 feet in length and able to carry a thousand passengers. 'Each vessel has a restaurant, also a tea room and two fully licensed Bars on board. There are sun lounges, spacious open decks and covered accommodation is available for all passengers. The steamers are the largest, fastest and most modern of their type afloat'.

On a day as calm and warm as that on which I had made the crossing in the now distant-seeming summer of the Thirties, I joined several hundred other holiday-makers aboard the *Bristol Queen*. This time, as soon as I reached the Marisco Tavern, I set out to walk the length of the island: along its west coast past the Battery, from which a gun was once fired as a fog warning, and the deep clefts known as the Earthquake, to Punchbowl Valley and the Half and Threequarter walls. From the North Light I came back along the track that runs the length of the island closer to the east side — and knew when I reached the tiny village again that I had still seen hardly anything. The place remained enigmatic, its innumerable features full of history.

I went back to London wanting to know more. Two hundred yards from the publisher's office where I worked was the British Museum. I had a ticket to the Reading Room; as part of my job I sometimes needed to work there. While waiting for the books I had requested to be brought from the miles of shelves hidden away behind the great circular wall of the domed Reading Room, I had often looked at books on Devon available on the open reference shelves. As a result I had written several essays, including a long one on Barnstaple which, many years later, formed the nucleus of a full-length book about the town. At that time the two bound volumes of the REPRINT OF THE BARNSTAPLE RECORDS introduced me to the name of John Roberts Chanter (1810-1895), a Bideford - born solicitor and keen antiquarian. With a Barnstaple schoolmaster, Thomas Wainwright, Chanter had rescued a mass of documents

Plate 1

Devil's Slide

concerning the town's past that were being allowed to rot away in damp conditions. Together they transcribed these valuable archives, translating from medieval French or Latin as necessary, and publishing their work, in the first instance, in the 'North Devon Journal'.

Chanter was a member of the Devonshire Association, which held its first formal meeting in Exeter in 1862. On the Reading Room shelves were the bound volumes of its Transactions, one for every year since its foundation. In the cumulative index I found that in August, 1871, at the Association's meeting at Bideford under the presidency of Charles Kingsley, Chanter had read a paper, 'A History of Lundy Island'. Like many of the papers published in the Transactions, it is lengthy, running to about 27,000 words, or a third of the length of an average modern novel. It would have taken about three hours to read aloud. Possibly Chanter condensed it somewhat for his audience.

Six years later he brought out the monograph as a small book, extended and revised. In his preface he remarked that the great interest 'evinced by visitors to North Devon, as to this romantic and remarkable island, has led to much enquiry about its history and peculiarities, which it is hoped the present volume will meet in a popular form'.

Usefully, in chapter one, he devoted several pages to an account of his sources. He found a 'valuable but diffusive paper, contributed by G. Steinman Steinman Esq., to a periodical called COLLECTANEA TOPOGRAPHICA about forty years since'. This was called simply 'Some Account of the Island of Lundy', and it would be interesting to know what had drawn Steinman to search the Patent Rolls, Hundred Rolls, Close Rolls, a long series of inquisitions post mortem and other medieval records to trace the history of the holders of Lundy from 1199 to the early 19th century. He was a member of the Oxford University Genealogical Society, had written a history of Croydon and was living, when he published his essay on Lundy, at Norwood.

Chanter also detailed 'what may be termed the literature of

Lundy', from the massive topographical poem POLYOLBION, in which Michael Drayton (1563-1631) devotes several hundred verses to discussing whether Lundy belongs to England or Wales, to Philip Gosse's record of his visit to the island in 1852.

Chanter took his original listeners, and later readers, on an anti-clockwise tour of the island, making it sound as though he was writing from personal observations and knowledge. This is remarkable because it seems that he never visited Lundy, much less walked round it noting the physical features he details. According to A. E. Blackwell[2] he spent a long time researching in the North Devon Athenaeum, Barnstaple, and was greatly helped by the Rev. H. G. Heaven, the son of William Hudson Heaven who then owned Lundy. Rev. Heaven stayed for three weeks at Chanter's house on Fort Hill, Barnstaple, and provided ample first-hand material.

After discovering Chanter's monograph I thought I might try to write something about Lundy, and made a start, but at about that time - 1950 - a book on the island, TEMPESTUOUS ISLE, was published[3]. There would be no room for another one for a long time, I thought, and turned to other things.

When, after many years, I returned to live in north Devon, it was to a village almost a dozen miles nearer Exmoor than the one in which I grew up. Yet even here, a hill nearby is high enough to offer a view of part of Barnstaple Bay — and often a dark bar can be seen on its horizon. Distinct or blurred, visible or invisible, according to the vagaries of the weather it predicts, it is still Lundy, a place of fascination.

Chapter Two

Lundy: so small an island. so long and often violent a history. It not only stands alone, unlike so many of the islands lying in groups around the western and northern coasts of Britain — the Isles of Scilly, the Hebrides, the Orkneys and Shetlands — but its position, commanding the approaches to the seaboards of north Devon and Somerset and South Wales, its steep high cliffs with only one reasonably accessible and easily defended landing place, gave it for centuries a value to lawless men.

Archeologists, who since the Second World War have carried out a good deal of excavation work on Lundy, provide useful guesses about the earliest inhabitants. The discovery of collections of microliths, the small worked flints used by men of the Stone Age to tip their spears, may indicate that a hunting group spent time there during the Mesolithic period, when frozen northern seas left large areas of dry land, so that what are now offshore islands were part of the mainland of Britain, and Britain itself was joined to the European land mass. Sunken forests extend westwards around the shores of Barnstaple Bay far beyond today's low tide line. Men may have hunted deer and other animals in the wide lowlands now deep under water. Then, Lundy would have stood high, a great granite plateau, a place, perhaps, of awe.

From later eras hut circles survive, but again, dating exactly when their makers lived offers no scholarly certainties, although pottery has been found which suggests that some were built in the Bronze Age[1].

That some Celts lived and farmed on the island there seems no doubt: the stone dwellings they built, and the small fields they ploughed, have left their traces in several parts of the island, and it is thought that they were still living there during the centuries after the Roman occupation of Britain. Although the Romans seem to have shown little interest in the northern part of Devon, their ships must sometimes have passed Lundy as they sailed up the channel leading to the river they knew as Sabrina to their settlement at Abonae, now Seamills, and even possibly on as far as Glevum (Gloucester). In the second century A.D. the geographer Ptolemy named Hartland Point the Promontory of Hercules. Chanter observes that he 'incidentally mentions, under the name of Heraclea, an island corresponding to Lundy'; centuries later Richard of Cirencester followed his lead, referring to 'Insula Herculea'.

More importantly, two Roman fortlets, or signal stations, were built one on either side of what is now Lynmouth, at Martinhoe and Old Barrow. It is said that their purpose was to keep an eye on the defiant tribesmen of South Wales, the Silures, but this would have been a difficult task: the Bristol Channel is more than fifteen miles wide at that point, and the Welsh coast is as often half-obscured in haze, mist or rain as is Lundy. However, Aileen Fox suggests that these little forts 'were built and maintained by troops who probably were landed in nearby coves on the rocky coast; the isolated garrisons would need to establish friendly relations with the native people in the many small hillforts in the neighbourhood'.[2]

For all that, Lundy was evidently not regarded as worth occupying by any Roman force: at least no archaeological finds have been made to suggest it.

When the last of the legions had been recalled to the defence of the crumbling empire in the first part of the fifth century A.D., the next visitors to western Britain were more peaceably inclined: they were the Celtic Christian missionaries from Ireland and Wales to whom the early Church accorded sainthood. A number of Cornish and Devon churches were dedicated to them, and some villages bear their names. At least one such missionary apparently settled on Lundy, and must have arrived hazardously in a very small boat. (Medieval hagiographers claimed that some of the holy men made miraculous sea crossings in various places on mill stones, or even large leaves, and it has been assumed that what they actually sailed in were coracles.) He remains nameless, but must have made converts. According to K. S. Gardner, although it is not known whereabouts the islanders then lived, it is possible to be fairly certain where they were buried: on the west side of Lundy's highest point, Beacon Hill. Four inscribed Christian memorial stones from the fifth or sixth centuries and one thought to be somewhat later have come to light. In 1923 it was noticed that a stone dug up some 18 years earlier, when Amelia Heaven's grave was being prepared, bore an inscription, deciphered as 'IGERNI . . . ITIGERNI' (the final I in each word lies vertically). It is surmised that this read originally as something like 'CONTIGERNI FILI TIGERNI' or 'The stone of Contigernus son of Tigernus', Tigernus meaning chief in the old Celtic language. In 1962 a second inscribed stone was found bearing a cross within a circle and the letters 'O/P/TIMI', translated as 'To the best one'. The following year two stones were found; one bore the words 'REST/EUTA', thought to be a woman's name, and the other 'POTIT(I)', 'The stone of Potitus'.

In the late Sixties an area of Beacon Hill was excavated. It had already revealed a small Iron Age settlement, with circular stone-walled huts that yielded many fragments of pottery. Now some thirty cist graves were found, although all traces of their occupants — even the teeth — had been dissolved in Lundy's acid soil. These indicate the existence of a small Christian community during the three or four centuries between the ending of Roman power on the mainland and the arrival of Saxon colonists there.

Nothing has so far been found to show who, if anyone, lived on the island for several centuries after the little Christian cemetery ceased to be used. Possibly some group of Scandinavian sea raiders carried off or killed the islanders and any farm animals they had, and no one dared to re-inhabit the place while that danger lasted. A happier possibility is that the community withdrew in good time to the comparative safety of Wales, or to what until the late medieval period was known as West Wales, in other words Cornwall.

Yet the Norsemen were well aware of Lundy and its wildlife; it was they, after all, who named it Puffin Island, and the first known documentary record of the name Lundy occurs in the Orkneyingasaga, written between 1139 and 1148.[4]

The Saxons, spreading out across southern England, reached Devon by the late 7th century. The Domesday survey shows that they had farms and settlements in many places in north Devon. The most substantial of these was one of the burghs set up by King Alfred to defend the coasts against the Danes, referred to in the Burghal Hideage of about 919 as Pilton-with-Barnstaple. Yet whether any Saxons sailed down the Taw, or out of the harbour of Alfreincombe (Ilfracombe) to visit Lundy, or spend time there, cannot be told; no evidence of their presence has been found.

Moreover there is no entry for Lundy in Domesday, which suggests that in the 11th century it was uninhabited, or regarded as of so little value that no Norman lord sought the Conqueror's permission to add it to his feudal holdings on the mainland, and therefore, at the time the Domesday survey was taken, in 1086, the Norman clerks saw no reason to hazard a crossing to what they may have supposed was a barren rock.

Nevertheless, by the early 12th century a family of Norman descent had established itself on Lundy, and for the next six centuries the island would be a base for men who were often violent and almost always outside the law.

In fact the first reference to Lundy in English historical documents, occurring in 1154, less than a century after the Conquest, concerns some kind of rebellious behaviour on the part of the incomer who made the island his stronghold, Sir Jordan de Marisco. (THE DICTIONARY OF NATIONAL BIOGRAPHY observes that the name Marisco, 'translated, is simply Marsh, as common in England in the middle ages as the marshes from which it is derived, and the compilers of the pedigree of the family of Mountmorris, or Montmorency, have caused much confusion by importing into their schemes the names of all persons of any note who were known by that common appellation, or one at all like it'.)

Sir Jordan had tenuous royal connections by marriage. His wife, Agnes, was a daughter of Hamelin Plantagenet. Hamelin was an illegitimate son of Geoffrey of Anjou, whose legitimate son, Henry, became Henry II of England, first of the Plantagenet line, taking his father's badge, the *planta genista* or broom, as his own. Perhaps Jordan presumed too much on his distant connection with the king; perhaps he had royal ambitions, or saw Lundy as a tiny kingdom that could become a stepping stone to something larger. Perhaps, like so many of his successors, he simple enjoyed indulging in buccaneering adventures. Whatever his actions or motives, Henry declared Lundy forfeit, and granted it to the Knights Templars.

It proved a nugatory gift. The Templars, established early in the twelfth century as the Order of Poor Knights, dedicated to protecting pilgrims on the dangerous road from Jaffa to Jerusalem, were rapidly becoming a very rich organisation, receiving donations of money and land throughout Christendom, but they were unable to obtain possession of Lundy: Sir Jordan stayed put, and defied them.

Nearly half a century passed. King John, acceding in 1199, confirmed the grant of Lundy, which the Latin deed sets at the mouth of the Severn between Tenby and Barnstaple ('in ore Sabrini fluminis inter Tinbeth et Bardestapulam'). By this time it was Sir Jordan's son William who held Lundy, and he was hardly more amenable to royal command than his father had been. He evidently raided places on the mainland, and in 1203 the Sheriff of Somerset recorded that he had received forty marks levied in the form of hideage (tax raised on land holdings) for the defence of the coasts of Devon and Cornwall against William de Marisco, as well as the sum of £47.16s paid on behalf of William de Briwere, or Brewer, who held properties in Devon. Whether these considerable sums for the time were used to pay for a successful sortie against Marisco does not appear; however they may have been, and he may have subsequently made his peace with the king, as he was in sufficient favour to be put in charge of the royal galleys. For all that, he must have been able to hold on to Lundy, as the Templars did not take charge of it and perhaps eventually complained, as in 1213 the king awarded them ten pounds in compensation.

Yet Marisco's rebellious streak must have remained. Professor Powicke, whose paper 'Henry Clement and the Pirates of Lundy' offers a helpful unravelling of the complexities and perplexities of the Marisco family's activities in the first half of the thirteenth century, observes that 'He was a naval administrator in King John's service, and he joined the rebels who had supported Louis of France during the war of 1215-17. He had put his wife, sons and daughters on Lundy Island and gone to sea against his king. The island was captured but restored to him, with his family, in November, 1217'.

King John had died, unlamented, in 1216, and been succeeded by his nine-year-old son Henry III. During Henry's minority the kingdom was governed by a regency council headed by William the Marshal. It was therefore the latter who restored the island to Marisco, who must have been a remarkably plausible man to manage to cajole this powerful lord — as he had earlier somehow cajoled King John — into exercising leniency. The fact that he was a person of some standing, a knight holding lands in Somerset as well as Lundy, would have cut no ice in court circles. Nevertheless he was not only permitted to hold on to Lundy but, in 1222, to add to whatever defences he may be assumed to have installed there. On his lordship Camley, south of Bristol, he had some mangonels. A mangonel was a military device, a kind of powerful catapult used for hurling objects, usually large stones, at an enemy. The Sheriff of Somerset agreed to the transfer of these to Lundy.

Exactly when he died is not known. However, according to Professor Powicke, he was the brother of Geoffrey de Marisco who held land in several counties in Ireland, a man of wealth and importance who had three times been justiciar (chief political and judicial officer) of Ireland. Yet he, and his son, another William, were to make the name of Marisco notorious among their contemporaries, and cause it to be remembered long after their dishonoured deaths.

Chapter Three[1]

In 1234 Geoffrey de Marisco, formerly justiciar of Ireland, and his son William were each fined 3,000 marks and imprisoned for their part in a rising in Ireland led by Richard Marshal, Earl of Pembroke, son of William the Marshal who had acted as regent during Henry III's minority. Released towards the end of the year they travelled to London — possibly to establish themselves in better favour with the king. In May, 1235, a cleric named Henry Clement came to London as a messenger from Geoffrey's successor as justiciar, Maurice Fitzgerald. He lodged at Westminster at a house owned by a surgeon opposite the gates of the king's palace. One night, when King Henry was in residence, a band of armed men rode up to Clement's lodging, smashed their way in and murdered him. The king was naturally incensed that such a crime should be committed at his very doors. The murderers were at once reported to be followers or associates of the Mariscos, who both fled, Geoffrey to the sanctuary of the Knights Hospitallers in Clerkenwell and William to Lundy. Three weeks later Geoffrey was pardoned but ordered to pay a large fine in addition to the one already levied against him. His lands and castles in Ireland were seized. He died a few years later — in exile and misery, according to the 13th century monk-historian Matthew Paris:[2] banished from England for non-payment of his fines, driven from Scotland (where he may for a time have sought refuge with King Alexander II) and disinherited in Ireland.

Geoffrey's son William evidently made Lundy his base, despite the fact that, as has been said, it was at that time held by his cousin, 'William son of Jordan' and thus grandson of the rebel who had joined supporters of Louis of France in 1215. This cousin, who can only recently have taken charge of the island on the death of his father Jordan, was quick to dissociate himself from the alleged murderer of Henry Clement, and was granted permission to leave the island 'come to England and stay there and retire from there; grant to him also that merchants may safely come and go from his said island as they used to do; and mandate accordingly to all bailiffs'[3]. This might suggest that he had been living a peaceable life, using the island as some sort of trading station, in which case the irruption of his outlawed Irish cousin would have been most unwelcome. However, at the time of the Irish rising he too had been with his great-uncle Geoffrey, and *his* castles and lands in Ireland were forfeit until October, 1237; it may in fact have been necessary for him to retire to the family's estate near Huntspill in Somerset for a year or two.

Professor Powicke suggests that the supposedly murderous 'William son of Geoffrey' may have spent some time in Scotland, like his father, and acquired Scottish supporters who 'put to sea with galleys and were preying upon merchants and others crossing from Ireland to England. They had attacked and taken merchants of Bristol, Dublin and Drogheda, killing some, wounding others and holding others to grievous ransom'. Yet with his family's apparent ability to evade arrest, William de Marisco remained at liberty, even though some of the king's ships were said to have assembled at Portsmouth ready to seek him out. Moreover he managed to collect £120 from the unfortunate merchants in ransom.

He was now more than ever an outlaw. Even if piracy was the only means left to him to provide for himself and his followers, the killing of harmless traders could not be excused. Though he was always to maintain that he was innocent of the murder of Henry Clement, his bloodthirsty piracy would have deepened suspicion of his earlier guilt.

The next crime of which he was accused went far beyond anything he had done so far, at least in the eyes of society and the law: it was attempted regicide.

In September, 1238, Henry III, now a man of thirty-three, on progress around his kingdom, was at Woodstock. A man-at-arms arrived and was admitted to the king's presence, whereupon he behaved in a manner that might well have led to his summary execution. Matthew Paris's chronicle (in Powicke's translation from the medieval Latin) tells the story:

'On the morrow of the nativity of the Blessed Mary (9th September, 1238) a certain man-at-arms, a man of some education, came to the king's court at Woodstock. Pretending to be mad, he said to the king: "Resign to me the kingdom which you have unjustly usurped and long detained". And he added that he had the mark of royalty on his shoulder. When the king's servants ran upon him, intending to beat him and drive him away from the king's presence, the king checked them, saying "Let him alone in his folly". But in the middle of the night, the madman climbed into the king's sleeping chamber by the window, a naked knife in his hand, and came to the king's bed. He did not find him and was perplexed. He looked for him in various parts of the chamber. By the providence of God the king was with the queen. One of the queen's damsels, Margaret Biset, happened to be on duty. She was reciting her psalter by the light of a candle, for she was devout. When she saw the madman searching every corner so that he could kill the king, shouting wildly, she was astounded and began to scream. The servants were awakened and came running in haste. They broke down the door which the burglar had barred, overbore his resistance, seized him, bound him with chains and put him to the torture. At length he confessed that he had been sent by William, son of Geoffrey of Marisco, to slay the king in the manner of the Assassins. He asserted that others also were concerned in the crime.'

Aspects of this report are strange, beginning with the king's tolerant dismissal of the unknown man as a harmless fool. Obvious questions occur. Even given that medieval monarchs not infrequently made themselves accessible to comparatively humble subjects, who might approach with a plea, complaint or even a gift, one may wonder what reason the stranger gave for wanting audience with Henry. What did he mean by 'the mark of royalty on his shoulder'? — knightly dubbing, or something more? How did he know which window belonged to the room in which he expected to find the king sleeping? Finally, in identifying William de Marisco as the man who sent him, was he telling the truth or, under the agonies of torture, merely calling up at random the name of a man who was known as an outlaw already accused of a murder close to the king's palace? *Was* the would-be assassin in fact deranged, a soldier suffering from delusions? He evidently arrived at Woodstock in a kamikaze mood; he is said not to have cared what happened to himself, as long as he achieved his purpose. Why should he have thought in this way, if he was merely carrying out the wishes of another man?

In his youth, William de Marisco had been in the king's service, becoming a member of the royal household in 1224, with a salary of forty marks a year. It is possible that he conceived a dislike of the young monarch, who would have been only a child when William left Ireland to join his court. Certainly his later actions in Ireland had been disloyal — and had earned him heavy penalties. He apparently saw himself as outlawed unjustly, as he protested to the day of his death that he had not caused the murder of Henry Clement. Certainly if he planned the king's death — from which he could hardly have expected to benefit — he chose a poor instrument in the oddly-behaved man-at-arms who made the noisy and inept attack at Woodstock.

Even after the latter had been put to death, no one was able to capture William de Marisco. He did not immediately take refuge on Lundy again, it seems; soon after the attempt on the king's life he was thought to be in Kent, and at a later time may have been in Wales: the Abbot of Margam was reprimanded for giving shelter to him and his men.

Yet he must often have used Lundy as his base for the continued piracy that alone would have made him a wanted man. In the words of Matthew Paris he made 'sudden irruptions on the adjacent lands, spoiling and injuring the realm by land and by sea, and native as well as foreign merchants in various ways.' Some noblemen who sailed close to Lundy on their way from Ireland must have decided to take a good look at possibilities of access, and concluded that they were poor; they reported to King Henry that 'the said William and his followers could not be surprised except by stratagem.' Three of William's men were arrested in December, 1241, by the Sheriff of Devon, and his wife Matilda, the niece of the archbishop of Dublin, was arrested the following month and imprisoned in Gloucester castle. (She was to be released, once her husband was dead, and eventually allowed to regain possession of her castles in Ireland.)

Finally a baron from Norfolk was sent to Devon to achieve by stratagem, as recommended, the capture of William de Marisco. Perhaps it was thought that someone from far away would show a resolution hitherto lacking. Thus in May, 1242, the East Anglian trouble-shooter, with the help of other knights and a dozen men-at-arms, managed to end Marisco's reign on Lundy.

'In a later copy of his chronicle Matthew Paris added a story that William was betrayed by one of his men, whom he had detained on the island against his will. The rocks protecting the place could be scaled at only one point, and William imprudently set this man to guard the weak spot. It was a misty day, and William was sitting at meat when the king's men came.'[4] How typical of the island's weather, that a mist, on a day in May, should have made things easier for the attacking force!

Marisco and his followers were taken first to Bristol and then to London. He and his more important men were imprisoned in the Tower; others went to Newgate and the Fleet. The authorities seem to have been almost neurotically anxious that the prisoners should not somehow, even now, escape, and ordered them to be kept in chains, heavily guarded, in the most secure places. In July they were tried and condemned to death.

Matthew Paris asserts that even on the eve of execution, William 'constantly affirmed, invoking the judgement of God, that he was free from and utterly guiltless of the crime of high treason charged against him, and the same of the death of the before-mentioned clerk, i.e. Clement; and that his only motive for withdrawing to the island had been by avoiding to turn aside the anger of the King, which by whatever judicial expiation, or other humiliation, it had always been his first wish to appease; but when he fled to the island, and called some friends to his assistance, he was driven, as he said, to support his wretched existence on necessaries snatched from every quarter.'

The execution of Marisco and his sixteen followers is all too graphically described by Paris. Marisco's body was dishonoured by a barbarity then apparently introduced for the first time, though it was to be enthusiastically practised for several centuries afterwards — drawing, disembowelling, and quartering. (Even as late as 1685 those condemned to death by Judge Jefferies at the Bloody Assizes were drawn and quartered after hanging. A Huguenot refugee who landed at Barnstaple in December, 1685, spoke of seeing the heads and quarters of those executed 'exposed on towers, gates and crossroads, looking absolutely like a butcher's shop'.) The quarters of Marisco and his men were sent to the four principal cities in the kingdom 'by that pitiable spectacle to strike terror in all beholders'.

King Henry took Lundy into his own hands. A partly built galley found on the shore was transferred to Ilfracombe for completion — early evidence of Ilfracombe's tradition of ship building.[5] (It would be interesting to know how Marisco managed to obtain timber for building not only this galley, but for other needs, such as beams, doors, benches, tables and perhaps rough bed frames in whatever dwellings he may have had built to house his men. Branches, logs and tree-trunks washed up on the little beach would have been of only limited use, and Lundy was presumably as treeless then as it is now, so it must have been necessary to transport shiploads of wood from the mainland.

King Henry, who was in France, sent orders that Henry de Tracy, lord of the manor of Barnstaple, was to supervise the construction of a fortress on Lundy. Whatever buildings had been erected during the hundred years or so of Marisco occupation would have been rased to the ground, though much of the stone-work may well have been re-used. In the 1960s a 12th-13th century fortified enclosure was excavated north of the medieval cemetery on Beacon Hill; it 'showed evidence suggestive of demolition and was covered in a late 13th century/15th century midden, containing not only pottery and food remains but silver coinage of Venice and France as well as of

England, together with various stone tools and metal objects. The date and importance of such a site suggests that it was the defended homestead of the early Mariscos and the demolition by the latter half of the 13th century may be attributed to the period when Henry III built his own castle there in 1243 A.D.[6]

It is ironic that what may be regarded as an anti-Marisco stronghold has for so long been known as Marisco Castle.

Presumably the first Marisco introduced rabbits to the island, as other Normans introduced them to the mainland. Henry de Tracy initiated a rabbit-catching programme; no fewer than 2,500 were said to have been caught and sold, the proceeds being thriftily used towards the construction of the castle.

In 1245 Henry de Tracy was appointed governor of the island, to hold it during the king's pleasure, and to make what he could from it. For the next twenty years King Henry changed the governorship of the island several times. Henry de Tracy's successors were Robert de Walerond, appointed in 1250, Sir Ralph de Wyllyngton, appointed in 1255, and Humphrey de Bohun, who shortly before the king's death in 1272 was succeeded by the lord of Hartland, Sir Geoffrey Dynant.[7]

Two years after his accession, Edward I ordered a detailed survey of Lundy. The jurors appointed to carry this out were told that the island was only two miles long and a mile wide towards the south. There were about twenty acres of arable sown with oats or barley, five acres of meadow and not only pasture for 'eight oxen and twenty cows, with their offspring, for two years', but 68 head of cattle, four mares and a stallion with their offspring for two years and, amazingly, as many as 900 sheep . On top of that there were the inevitable rabbits; it was estimated that as many as 2,000 a year could be caught, 'bringing in 5s.6d. each 100 skins, because the flesh is not sold'. How the island could have supported such a remarkable quantity of stock — especially as the rabbits would presumably have nibbled a large share of the herbage — is difficult to comprehend. However, this survey indicates that successive governors of the island had ensured that it was farmed intensively during the past thirty years.

The island was well guarded; it was reported that 'in summer, even in time of peace, it is necessary to have fourteen servants and a constable to watch the defences of the island, and in winter ten servants'. Surprisingly, since the island's granite must surely have provided for all buildings since it was first occupied, it was stated that there was no quarrying stone.

After the difficulties experienced in Henry III's time it might have been supposed that no English monarch would allow a member of the Marisco family to take charge of Lundy — yet in 1281 Edward I granted the island, for the service of a mere tenth part of a knight's fee, to Sir William de Marisco, described as 'son and heir of Jordan, son and heir of Geoffrey sometime viceroy of Ireland.' Did Edward, preoccupied for so much of his reign with subduing the understandably resentful people of Wales, suppose that Sir William would be useful as a defender of the approaches to the Welsh coast?

This last William died in 1284. His son John died only five years later, leaving a son, Herbert. Herbert's stepmother Olivia, John's second wife, claimed the island as her dower, and a lawsuit resulted, though not until 1321, fourteen years after the accession of Edward II. The island meanwhile had been taken over by Sir John de Wyllyngton, a descendant of the Sir Ralph who had been governor from 1255 to 1260; adopting Marisco tactics, he held it by force and refused Herbert access. Even when Sir John became implicated in a rebellion, and his lands forfeited, the unfortunate Herbert was unable to regain Lundy, as the king gave the island and all Wyllyngton's holdings to the last of his favourites, Hugh le Despencer the younger.

A new survey was taken as part of the general inquisition on Wyllyngton's sequestered estates. This shows that Sir John may have had some justification in defending the island against strangers, as there had been a raid by Scots (or more probably French) pirates, which had destroyed the farmhouse attached to the castle, as well as the rabbit warren and the gannets' nesting place. The survey makes it clear that at some time Herbert had in fact administered the island, since there were said to be eight tenants who held their land and tenements 'by a certain charter of Herbert de Mareis granted them for the term of their lives, who pay fifteen shillings yearly.' There was also a tenant who was keeper of the gannets during their breeding season 'for which service he will be quit of his rent of two shillings.'[8]

When in 1326 the misguided and largely ineffectual king, Edward II, was finally driven from his kingdom by a powerful conspiracy led by his queen, Isabella of France, and her lover Roger Mortimer, he is said to have hoped to find refuge on Lundy. Accompanied by the man he had presented it to, Hugh le Despencer, he reached Chepstow and set sail in a small boat. The weather was not kind; he was driven to put back to the coast of Glamorgan. Captured and taken to Berkeley Castle, he was put to death in a particularly vicious manner.

Sir Thomas de la More's account of the life and death of Edward II (written in fact by Geoffrey Baker c.1350)[9] describes Lundy as 'two miles in length every way' and gives a glowing account of its attractions. It abounded in pleasant pastures, as well as rabbits, pigeons and gannets; it was well supplied with water from fresh springs, and moreover it had been well stocked up with wine, oil, honey, corn, malt, salted fish, meat and pitcoal. This suggests that le Despencer had made the island ready to receive the king, and had assured him that it would be easy to defend. He had certainly taken care that the temporarily disgraced John de Wyllington had given up his right and title to the island, according to Dugdale, and he had presented a priest, Walter de Bitte or Bot, to the church of St. Helen's there in 1325, so he obviously interested himself in the life of the island.[10]

After Edward II's death Sir John de Wyllyngton was restored to his estates as Lord Wyllyngton. In a court hearing at Westminster in October, 1332 'as to the Castle of Lunday and ten messuages, ten ploughlands, ten acres of meadow, 10,000 acres of heath, sixty shillings rent in Lunday and the advowson of the church of Lunday', Ralph, Lord Wyllyngton's son acknowledged the right of William de Monte Acuto (Montacute, first Earl of Salisbury) to the castle, tenements and advowson and gave them up to him at the court 'to have and to hold to William and his heirs of the chief lords of that fee by the services which belong to the said castle, tenements and advowson for ever', for which William gave him two hundred pounds. (An additional nought seems to have attached itself to the acreage of heathland.)

Yet in June, 1333, again at Westminster, and in October, 1334 at York, William Montacute paid two other 'deforciants', or claimants, Hugh le Despencer and Stephen de Marisco, what were for the times large sums of money: 1,000 marks of silver to Hugh, and three hundred pounds sterling to Stephen, who thus appears as the very last of his name to profit from Lundy — though, breaking with family tradition, this profit was a legal one.[11]

An 18th century engraving of the Marisco Castle from Grose's ANTIQUITIES.

Chapter Four

For some reason William Montacute's payment of two hundred pounds to Ralph Wyllyngton in 1332 does not seem to have been
binding: at least when Lord Wyllyngton died only five years later the usual inquisition post mortem recorded that Sir John Luttrell had been holding Lundy from him by military service, and when Lord Wyllyngton's nephew and heir died in 1347 the island was again said to be held on feudal terms, by one knight's fee, by the Earl of Salisbury.

The Earl's granddaughter, Elizabeth Montacute, married Sir Guy de Brian. By that time there seems to have been no doubt that it was in the possession of her family and, as Salisbury's heiress, she had a right to it. On her husband's death in 1390 it was left to their two young daughters, but once again there were disputes. Legal wrangling lasted ten years, but at last Lundy was granted to the elder daughter; her descendants for several generations continued to hold it until, as one of them had married James Butler, Earl of Ormonde, it was seized by Edward IV after Ormonde had been beheaded in 1461 for treason. It remained in royal hands for nearly two decades until Henry VII, in 1488, granted it to Thomas Earl of Ormonde, brother of the executed James. Through one of Thomas's daughters it became part of the estates of the St. Leger family of Annery, near Bideford.[1] However, a spendthrift Sir John St. Leger borrowed large amounts of money from his son-in-law, Sir Richard Grenville, using his property as security.

A. L. Rowse, in his biography of Grenville, observes that in 1577 St. Leger granted Grenville 'the fee simple of the island of Lundy. It is a very complicated and involved document by which the transfer takes place, and it makes pathetic reading, for behind its legal complications may be discerned the very human hope of the St. Legers some day to regain this strip of their patrimony. It is provided that if they perform their agreement to pay the sums of money owing, then they might re-enter into the possession of the Island and Manor. But they never did, and this is how Lundy came into the hands of the Grenvilles.[2]

Just two and a half centuries lie between the death of Edward II and the sale of Lundy to Sir Richard Grenville. In all that time it does not seem that any of the nobility and gentry, or their monarchs, who were proprietors of the island, actually visited the place — or if they did, no record of such a visit is known. Even those who prepared surveys from time to time seemed to have avoided seeing the island for themselves, or they could hardly have given such inaccurate reports of its measurements. The court cases of the 1330s, quoted earlier, show that it was then inhabited by ten households, and farmed on a modest basis.

There is no way of knowing what became of those ten peasant farmers and whatever families they may have had when, in the summer of 1348, the terrible pandemic of bubonic plague known as the Black Death reached the coast of Dorset and began to spread throughout Britain. Lundy's isolation may have offered protection, but any visiting seaman might have brought the infection before the danger was known.

The Rev. Boggis, in his history of the diocese of Exeter, includes Lundy's church of St. Helen among the 'posts that were filled up because they had been rendered void by death' during the years 1348-50.[3] However, if priests died as the result of the first outbreak of plague (there were four recurrences during the remainder of the 14th century) it might have been expected that, like so many of the lay population, they would do so comparatively quickly. Admittedly, delay in filling vacant livings may have been unavoidable, yet in the case of Lundy Sir Thomas de Wynkeleghe was not collated to the church on Lundy until 1350, and it is perfectly possible that his predecessor, Sir William de Tettewell, was moved elsewhere, or died of some cause other than plague.

So, although as has been said there are records of the men or women who held title to Lundy, there is a long silence concerning any ordinary inhabitants until in Tudor times the place begins to feature more and more often in reports of that perennial nuisance of the days of sail, piracy.

Attacks might be made by foreign — especially French — ships; they might be carried out by British buccaneers on foreign ships or on merchant ships belonging to their own country. For instance, in 1542 a French pirate called de Val seized Lundy and used it as a base from which to raid ships trading in western waters. As it was then in the hands of Sir James St. Leger, it may have been with the latter's help and encouragement that the men of Clovelly 'with small vesselles entred upon the isle, and fyrst toke the most parts of the men, and after toke the shipp, which lay in the rode before it.' By contrast Lord Seymour, who had been sent to the Isles of Scilly in 1547 to put down local pirates, not only conspired with them and took them over, but thought he might establish 'a sure and safe refuge' on Lundy. (He was executed in 1549.)[4]

All through the 1560s and 1570s English, and especially Cornish, privateers were haunting Lundy and the coasts of the west country. These men were of course outlaws, but there were pirates of another kind: those who sailed under letters of marque, which were in effect licences to prey on foreign ships — primarily those belonging to countries with which Britain happened to be at war, handing over a percentage of the booty to the Crown.

Elizabeth I, like monarchs before and after her, issued these documents. During her reign many ports in Devon and Cornwall sent out vessels to capture prizes on this basis, and very valuable some of them were. A number of sea captains of Barnstaple and Bideford enriched themselves by capturing Spanish vessels laden with such things as wine, ivory and precious metals. Richard Dodderidge, mayor of Barnstaple in 1589, owned a 100 ton ship, the *Prudence*, which one day in 1590 sailed up the Taw to Barnstaple quay 'having in her four chests of gold to the value of sixteen thousand pounds and divers chaines of gold with civet and other things of great value.'[6]

However, English venturers like Dodderidge did not have everything their own way. Privateers from the Mediterranean had been sailing north in increasing numbers. They captured British sailors, and sometimes seized women and children from coastal villages and sold them into slavery or demanded ransoms. Not long before the Spanish Armada put to sea, a collection was taken in Barnstaple to redeem captives out of Turkey (in fact Algeria: pirates from both Algiers and Tangier were often referred to as Turkish).[6] At about the same time William Bourchier, Earl of Bath, who had built a fine new house at Tawstock in 1574, ordered an attack to apprehend 'divers rovers and pirates at Londay'. The cost of this expedition was surprisingly modest, even for the late 16th century: borough funds were charged five shillings and five pence. The attack was successful; prisoners were brought back to Barnstaple and kept in the Quay Hall, with six men to watch them.[7]

Throughout the reigns of James I and Charles I, buccaneers both foreign and domestic continued to harry merchant ships unceasingly in the English Channel, the Bristol Channel and the Irish Sea. 'Between 1609 and 1616 no fewer than 466 British vessels were captured by Algerines and their crews enslaved'.[8]

In September, 1608, the Earl of Bath took the depositions of Barnstaple merchants who reported that their ships were being daily robbed at sea by pirates, mostly English ones, it would seem. One particularly bloodthirsty man was Thomas Salkeld. In the Calendar of State Papers for 1609 he appears as Sakell, one of four English freebooters who had taken a flyboat near Spain, but the following year an entry records that he 'went with his men and colours and took the island of Lundy in defiance of the king of England and wished His Majesty's heart upon the point of his sword, and called himself king of Lundy'. He captured several ships, shaved the heads of their crews 'and set them and the inhabitants at work building a quay and fortifications; afterwards he mustered them and, setting up a gallows, swore that unless they took the oath of allegiance to him as king of Lundy they should hang upon it.' Eventually a merchantman officer, George Escott, led a revolt of the prisoners, and Salkeld and his men at once ran away. His whole invading force was said by one witness to consist of only sixteen men and boys, but

Plate 2

Marisco Castle

another claimed that he had 130 volunteers and prisoners, had taken a number of ships, and was expecting to be joined by other pirates. Escott, an Appledore man, was granted a pension of eighteenpence a day for his action. Salkeld did not long survive; he was wounded in a sea fight and his body thrown overboard.[9]

The Privy Council, repeatedly petitioned during the reign of James I to take action, responded by demanding contributions towards the cost of fitting out a punitive expedition. Merchants felt that this was adding insult to injury, and yielded grudgingly. A fleet of eighteen ships sailed to the Mediterranean in October 1620, but achieved little.[10] Later the merchants and shipowners of all the principal ports from Barnstaple to Southampton united to complain that they could not trade, and had the expense of supporting the wives and children of captured sailors.

In 1625, the first year of Charles I's reign, the mayor and aldermen of Bristol reported to the Privy Council that three 'Turkish' pirates had surprised and taken Lundy, carrying off its inhabitants. According to one merchant, Nicholas Cullen, the pirates had spent a fortnight on the island; he claimed to have seen their ships lying in Lundy Roads.[11]

Three years later it was a French man-of-war that was seizing vessels off Lundy. A Captain Fogg, commanding HMS *St. James*, reported this in April, 1628, but by the following month had to admit that he had seen and heard nothing of the culprit.

Early in Charles I's reign the Navy was making some attempt to deal with such attacks. In 1627 a class of small fast ships was built. These, numbered from one to ten, were named the Lion's Whelps, and the State Papers contain many references to them. They often operated in western waters. However, by 1630 naval captains whose duties entailed convoy and patrol duties were evidently feeling increasingly frustrated. In June of that year Captain Richard Plumleigh (later Sir Richard), admiral of the fleet on the coast of Ireland, probably spoke for them all when he complained that 'Egypt was never more infested with caterpillars than the Land's End with Biscayners. On 23rd instant, there came out of St. Sebastian's twenty sail of sloops. Some attempted to land on Lundy, but were repulsed by the inhabitants'.[12] (The latter were said to have 'hurled boulders down the cliff and happily slaughtered the lot of them'). As long as he plied to and fro, the pirates kept away, but as soon as he put in for provisions they were as bad as ever. Their ships must have been smaller than those commanded by Plumleigh, as they were able to 'run in among the rocks', where pursuit was impossible.

(It is somewhat surprising, incidentally, to learn that after the disastrous raid of 1625, Lundy had been re-inhabited — but evidently by people who were better prepared to beat off attackers.)

During the summer and autumn of 1632 Captain Plumleigh was kept busy. In July he was ordered to 'hasten him away for Ireland and the Severn, where pirates swarm'. The mayor of Bristol told the master of the Ninth Whelp that 'some had come to him that were taken about Lundy by an English pirate, who robbed them of all they had' (but set them ashore afterwards, presumably, to tell the tale). One noted English pirate of this time was a Robert Nutt; having more than one ship under his command he enjoyed referring to himself as Admiral Nutt, while one of his followers styled himself Vice Admiral. Captain Plumleigh reported from Plymouth Sound that he intended to sail for the Severn, 'where he hears that Nutt's vice admiral lies expecting the return of Irish merchants from the fair' (St. James' Fair),[13] In September he caught up with Nutt and his companions and 'bestowed on Nutt's ship ten great shot, but they escaped, being clean and light ships. He regretted that he had not had one of the Whelps, as he was sure he could have taken the pirate with them. The wind had not been favourable, or he might have surprised Nutt at anchor.' He was making for Lundy and Caldey, 'which are the pirates' dens.'[14]

In June of the following year, Captain Plumleigh sent the Ninth Whelp into the Severn to clear it of pirates, whereupon 'they betook themselves to Lundy and the Welsh islands'.[16] A month after this Sir Bernard Grenville, owner of Lundy, reported 'a great outrage committed by a Spanish man-of-war of Biscay'. Eighty men had landed, quickly overcome the islanders' resistance, killed a man named Mark Pollard, bound the others and carried off all the best provisions they could find; they also robbed a pinnace belonging to a George Rendall, who happened to be lying off Lundy, and made off with his money and provisions.[16] In August Sir Richard Plumleigh captured a Biscayner, though not, it seems the same one.

Two years later Captain Sir John Pennington was reporting to the Admiralty that he had not been able to hear of any 'Turks', only a small Biscay man-of-war or two, with two or three shallops, 'which lie pilfering between Lundy and Mounts Bay.' (A shallop was a large heavy boat with one or more masts, sometimes carrying guns.) They robbed small trading vessels sailing between Ireland, Wales and the west coast of England. As far as he knew they only stole food 'yet that makes great noise among small men.' He suggested that the solution would be 'to call in question all such as harbour them, or furnish them with victuals, and secondly to have two or three small vessels to go with the fleet for hunting out these picking rogues.' He too complained that the pirates could lie among the rocks close to the shore. Somewhat surprisingly, he added that people living along the coasts not only harboured and provisioned the freebooters but warned them of the approach of naval vessels.

The people of Lundy, however, were clearly not disposed to help pirates, and must have lived in a constant state of vigilance, yet two contemporary Devon-born writers, Thomas Westcote and Tristram Risdon, who both included some mention of Lundy in their topographical accounts of the county, made no mention of piratical attacks. It seems doubtful whether either actually visited the island, though both certainly implied that they had done so. Writing in 1620 Westcote, having described Northam, went on: 'Here, had I not casually cast my eye on the Severn Sea and seen an island belonging to this county, I had struck sail and cast anchor. But while our bark is afloat it is four hours sailing from hence with a good wind: let us view it. That it hath been tilled in former times the furrows testify yet plainly but what commodities came thereof is not known, neither will any man try again; there is little hope of profit. The most profit that is now made of it is by hogs, conies, and sea-fowl.' when the birds were breeding, he added, "in some places you shall hardly know where to set your foot but on eggs.'[18]

Risdon's version, written a few years later, begins by describing Lundy as lying in a bay 'between Bagg Point and Harty . . . incircled with inaccessible clifts (sic) and rocks, on every side defending it, and not to be assaulted but in one or two places, and that dangerous, being in a manner impregnable. A fort it sometime had, the ruins thereof, and of St. Helen's chapel, are yet to be seen. It is plentifully served with fresh springs . . . The south part of this island is of an indifferent good soil, having a small island called Lamitor, now Rat Island, joined by a little nack of land, where sampier (samphire) groweth abundantly The north part is more barren, where standeth a rock, pyramid-wise, of a great height, called the Constable, keeping true centinal (sic). Horses, kine, sheep, swine and goats it affordeth, with store of conies; but their chief commodity is fowl, whereof there is so great an abundance which in the time of breeding, I have seen their eggs so thick on the ground, that unless you look your way, they must needs have been trodden on.'[19]

Camden, in his BRITANNIA, gives a picture of Lundy very similar to those of Westcote and Risdon, and John Thomas suggests that 'they were all based on, in part at least, one common source that was composed after Lundy fell to the Grenvilles in 1577.'[20]

The Grenvilles might have been expected to make determined efforts to protect Lundy from attack. However, it would not be surprising if Sir Richard Grenville took only a minimal interest in it; he may have felt for the time being it was no wholly his concern, as St. Leger might have been able to repay the loan for which it was security, and repossess it. More importantly, Grenville was too preoccupied with transatlantic voyages and his attempt to colonize Roanoke Island in Pamlico Sound, off the coast of what is now North Carolina, to care greatly for the smaller island so much nearer home.

However, three years after his death in 1591 his son Bernard was ordered by the Privy Council to fortify Lundy, but took no action. Two years later the Earl of Bath asked the Council to ensure that the island was made 'somewhat defensible, for if the enemy once take it, it will be a very hard thing without famine to remove him again'[21] the enemy then being Spain. In a letter written in April, 1596, Sir Bernard said, more or less, that he could not afford it, and would be glad if the Queen would pay for men to guard the island.[22] The council's reply was a mild form of official blackmail: 'if you neglect the place her Majestie shall have cause to take the Islande whollie into her own hands and make her owne profitt of it for the defence of the same.'[23]

It is possible that Sir Bernard responded by constructing a gun battery at the point on the east coast of the island near the Threequarter wall known as Brazen Ward. 'Pottery found here could well date from the 16th century. Traditionally the site has been regarded as of Civil War period, being ascribed to Lord Saye and Sele, but if the pottery is 16th century it may prove to be the work of the Grenvilles.'[24]

In 1631 Sir Bevil Grenville, Sir Bernard's son, certainly wanted to fortify Lundy. He abandoned plans to do so because an adviser, Sir John Eliot, warned him that only the Crown had the right to build such defences. But for this, the people of Lundy might have had a much easier time in the 1630s. In the next decade, the outbreak of the Civil War changed everything. Lundy was fortified, and garrisoned for the king — but not by a member of the Grenville family.

Chapter Five

In spite of the repeated seaborne alarms in the waters around Lundy during the first half of the seventeenth century, and the frequent attacks on the island itself, several men with strong personal reasons for avoiding society chose to retire there. The first was a member of an old north Devon family, the Bassets, who had lived at Heanton Court near Braunton since Henry VIII's time. In January, 1600, Sir William Pole, of Colcombe and Shute (1561-1635) author of THE DESCRIPTION OF DEVON, wrote to his uncle, Sir John Popham, lord chief justice, to warn him that Sir Robert Basset was reported to have resolved 'to have the Isle of Lundy, and to place there one Ansley, a malcontent, a Somersetshire man.' He asked to have the journey Sir Robert was about to undertake with a man called Hill (who apparently persuaded him to practise 'popery') prevented, and Hill arrested, to avoid 'the overthrow of the gentle nature of Sir Robert.' According to John Prince, in his WORTHIES OF DEVON, Basset was said to be 'by his grandmother, descended from the Plantagenets, and of the blood royal of England' and to have made some pretensions to the crown of England at the beginning of James I's reign. 'but not being able to make them good, he was forced to fly into France to save his head'.[1] From France he travelled on to Italy. From Pisa, writing to his brother, he said he wished with all his heart he was at Lundy 'in as poor case as I came from thence, where I would gladly spend my days in an obscure hermitage'.[2]

Sir Lewis Stukeley, Vice Admiral for Devon, withdrew to Lundy after his betrayal of his kinsman Sir Walter Raleigh had earned him the nickname 'Sir Judas'. Raleigh, a prisoner in the Tower after he had been implicated in a plot against James I in 1603, had been released in 1615 to undertake a voyage to Guiana whence, he claimed, he could bring back a shipload of gold for the king. He failed in this, and angered James by clashing with Spaniards at San Tomé. Landing at Plymouth, weary and in poor health, Raleigh set out for London to try to justify himself. Stukeley met him on the way, having been instructed to conduct him to the king. Learning that Raleigh had brought back a valuable cargo of tobacco, he went on to Plymouth and sold the cargo, taking the proceeds for himself. Raleigh was held in London under house arrest, still in the care of Stukeley, who affected compassion and sympathy for him at all times. It became clear to Raleigh that if he wanted to save his life he must — all too late — attempt to escape to France, where he knew he would be welcomed. Trustingly, he told Stukeley of his plans. The latter offered to go with him — and arranged for his arrest as they sailed down the Thames. At last recognizing that he had been betrayed, Raleigh offered only the restrained reproof, 'Sir Lewis, these actions will not turn out to your credit.'

Indeed they did not, and the payment Stukeley received was widely referred to as his thirty pieces of silver. When he complained to the king, the latter merely remarked that if he was to hang all who spoke ill of Stukeley, all the trees in his kingdom would not suffice.[3]

Stukeley was a nephew of Sir Richard Grenville, and as has been said, since the latter's death in 1591 Lundy had been in the possession of Sir Richard's son, Sir Bernard. Possibly Stukeley sought his permission to make to make the island a place of refuge until the widespread contempt he had aroused had lessened. Yet it would seem that guilt quickly induced dementia, and two years after Raleigh's execution he died 'a poor distracted beggar', as an early biography of Raleigh put it.

(It must be added that the DICTIONARY OF NATIONAL BIOGRAPHY maintains that the case against Stukeley 'lacks solid foundations', and that he had reason to hold a grudge against Raleigh for an injury he had done to his father in 1584.)

Throughout the Civil War, Lundy was held for the Royalist cause by one of the most unusual characters in its history, Thomas Bushell.[4] Born in 1594 in Gloucestershire, he had been taken into the household of the Lord Chancellor, Sir Francis Bacon, as a boy of fifteen. Bacon introduced him to the study of methods of prospecting for minerals, and mining them, which was to occupy him for the rest of his life.

Indulged by Bacon, he quickly acquired extravagant habits, which he never lost; but for a time he was protected from the consequences because his master paid off his creditors. He loved finery, and when he accompanied Bacon to court, James I commented on his gorgeous clothes.

In 1624, impeached for taking bribes, Bacon fell from favour. John Aubrey, whose BRIEF LIVES includes some account of Bushell, remarks 'T'was the fashion in those days for gentlemen to have their suits of clothes garnished with buttons. My Lord Bacon was then in disgrace, and his man Bushell having more buttons than usual on his cloaks, etc., they sayd that his lord's breech made buttons and Bushell wore them — from whence he was called buttoned Bushell.'[5]

However, Bushell withdrew from the world to live on the Isle of Wight, disguised as a fisherman. Although he returned for a short time to London, Bacon's death sent him into seclusion on another island, the Calf of Man. There, 'in obedience to my dead lord's philosophical advice, I resolved to make a perfect experiment upon myself for the obtaining of a long and healthy life, most necessary for such a repentance as my former debauchedness required, by a parsimonious diet of herbs, oil, mustard and honey.'

With the accession of Charles I his fortunes improved. He married Anne, widow of Sir William Waad, lieutenant of the Tower; she was able to bring him a substantial dowry, but Aubrey said he did not 'encumber himself' with his wife. Living at Enston in Oxfordshire he discovered a spring and a curiously-shaped rock in his grounds, and built a banqueting house over them, where he was able to entertain the king and, later, Queen Henrietta Maria, for whom he wrote a masque. By 1637 he had leased the mines of Cardiganshire and was working them with some success.

Although at the outbreak of the Civil War in 1642 Lundy was still the property of Sir Bevil Grenville, Bushell managed to obtain the king's appointment as governor of the island. It was evidently opportune: in debt as usual, he was not at all sorry to be out of reach of his creditors, who were becoming ill-natured, as he put it. He may well have previously considered Lundy as a possible place of refuge when on his way to visit the silver mines of Combe Martin. However, he declared his intention to 'stand upon my own strength and keep the Garrison of Lundy at my own charge, promising him (the king) either to die in the place, or that it should be the last Garrison surrendered.' To the credit of his not entirely disinterested loyalty, it was.

It is clear that he had been of very real use to Charles, as a letter written to him in June, 1643, shows; it lists his 'manie true services . . . in these times of trying a subject's loyalty.' These included raising the miners of Derbyshire for the royal life guard at the start of the war, supplying money from his own mint to pay the army, as well as providing a hundred tons of lead shot without payment and importing large quantities of ammunition from abroad.

Bushell liked Lundy, ' . . . it being a place of such privacy as my disposition is well known to affect, had not the troubles of these unhappy times made me more in love with.' Another, more practical consideration he mentions in a letter to a friend: ' . . . and for my retirement to Lundy, it is well known, the occasion was my affection to solitude, the pressing of my miners at Commartin, as also to prevent an ill inhabitant.'

Sir Bevil Grenville was killed fighting for the king at the battle of Lansdowne in 1643. His son, also Sir Bevil, who was to be created Earl of Bath in 1661 (the Bourchier title having lapsed) would therefore have inherited Lundy with other Grenville properties. However in 1645 William Fiennes, first Viscount Say and Seal, set up some claims to it, referring to it as his inheritance, which clearly it was not, though it seems that the Parliament forces had allowed him to buy it. He was a Puritan, and all his sons fought against Charles; his Cavalier enemies called him Old Subtlety. Clarendon says that he was 'of a prowde, morose, sullen nature', and that he lived 'narrowly and sordidly in the country, haveing conversation with very few, but such who had great malignity against the Church and State.'

He wrote to Bushell in February, 1646, offering to sell him the island for £3,000. Bushell had resisted attempts to storm or starve his garrison into submission, and ignored demands to give it up; he was certainly unlikely to have £3,000 to buy the island. He did make a tentative offer to swap it for some part of his Oxfordshire estate, but nothing more was heard of that.

At last, on 14th May, 1646, having decided that he could no longer hold out, he wrote to the king to ask for formal permission to surrender. Enclosing the most recent demand from Lord Saye, sent via the governor of Swansea, he refers to 'this Isle, being his lordship's known purchase.' Sir Thomas Fairfax, he said, had offered to help to restore his silver mines in exchange for delivering Lundy to Lord Saye. He reminded the king of his expenses: 'Your Majesty well knoweth how I have maintained Lundy at no other contribution but my own, and how cheerfully I have exposed my friends and my own credit for your services, as well as exhausted them in the discovery of the mines royall.' He asked leave to give up the island freely and quietly; if this was not granted he promised to remain and 'sacrifice both life and fortune.'

Two months later the king sent his reply from Newcastle;

'Bushell,

We have perused your letter, in which we find thy care to answer thy trust We at first reposed in thee. Now, the place is inconsiderable in itself, and yet may be of great advantage unto you in respect of your Mines, We do hereby give you leave to use your discretion in it, with the Caution, that you do not take example from Our selves, and be not over-credulous of vain promises, which hath made Us great, only in our sufferings, and will not discharge your debts.'

From Lundy on 24th February, 1648, Major Richard Fiennes, one of Old Subtlety's sons, wrote to Sir Thomas Fairfax, commander of the Parliamentary forces in the west, to report that the island had been given up. He referred to the fact that Bushell had visited the mainland six months earlier to negotiate with Fairfax in person. The

Plate 3

The East side of the island, looking north

garrison had evidently been short of food towards the end, not surprisingly after so long a siege, although it would have been possible to catch fish and grow vegetables and perhaps some cereal crops. Moreover the cattle and sheep that must have been on the island at the start would presumably have bred, though probably not fast enough for the appetites of the soldiers. Some of them, however, were said to have declined to eat horseflesh.

Bushell met Major Fiennes on the quay at Clovelly, but they had to spend fifteen days ashore before the wind was favourable for sailing to Lundy. The names of the garrison Fiennes found on the island are given in his report. Including Bushell, there are twenty-two, among them a Major Richard Pomeroy and a Lieutenant Oliver Brook. 'The morning tide following they took shipping for Ilford Combe, where he purposeth to imploy them in his chargeable adventures of recovering the distressed works of Commartyn Mynes and his other minerals in Wales.'

Fiennes ended his letter with a generous tribute: ' . . . this integrity of theirs, and the honesty of the governour, as also his publique imployment for minerals for the common good being confirmed by the country, makes me humbly present their names here underwritten as officers and souldiers of the last garrison, and men that have done the least of injuries notwithstanding their sad condition, which I wish for the president (precedent?) of others, they may be lookt on as the best of enemies that have conditions from the honourable Parliament and your Excellency.'

The terms of the treaty issued by Parliament concerning 'the delivering up of the isle of Lundy to the Lord Viscount Say and Seal or his assignees, by Mr. Thomas Bushell' stated that 'the delinquency of the said Thomas Bushell be taken off, and all sequestrations in respect thereof be discharged, and he and his assignees restored to all such rights as he or they had or ought to have in the mines of Devonshire, Wales and Cornwall, and to all other his estates and rights whatsoever; and that the men that were with him in the island, not being soldiers of estate and fortune, be pardoned and freed from delinquencies.'

It looks as though Bushell, after leaving Lundy, first sought help from Lewis Incledon, a Royalist who owned the mines at Combe Martin. King Charles wrote to Incledon on 26th October, 1648, saying that he had 'received a faire Character of your serviceable Endeavours advancing his (Bushell's) further discovery of the Mynes att Commartin in order to the publique good and having a sight of the Oare which we conceive lies there in vast proportions . . . We have thought fitt . . . to lett you know that We shall esteem it an acceptable service if . . . you add to his encouragements . . .'[6]

The unhappy king had only three more months before his execution. Bushell lived on until 1674, sometimes in trouble with Cromwell's followers during the Commonwealth period, often pursued by creditors. He seems to have retained his interest in mining, and his ability to raise loans to further it. 'He had the strangest bewitching way to drawe-in people (yea, discreet and wary men) into his projects that ever I heard of. His tongue was a chaine and drewe in so many to be bound for him and to be ingaged in his designs that he ruined a number,' Aubrey recorded.[7] Yet when he died in April, 1674 — one hundred and twenty pounds in debt, it was said — he was accorded burial in the cloisters of Westminster Abbey.

Lord Say withdrew from public affairs after the king's death, and chose to spend a few years on Lundy, apparently maintaining it as a garrison on behalf of Parliament. The captain of a Royalist privateer sent him a triumphantly impudent letter in March, 1651, boasting that 'Not far from that pretty island, whereof your Lordship is petty Prince' he had seized a small vessel carrying provisions for the garrison, and sold them 'dog cheap, viz. for £15 because I could not get more', though he had let the captain keep his ship, as he was a poor man.[8]

A tantalisingly brief remark in a letter written in about October, 1653, shows that Lord Saye was known to be there then. Discussing translations of French romances in one of her witty, elegant and lively letters to her future husband, the young Sir William Temple, Dorothy Osborne says that she has been told that Lord Saye 'has writ a romance since his retirement in the Isle of Lundy'. Regrettably the manuscript, if indeed it existed, has not survived.[9]

After the Restoration, Lord Saye took his seat in the House of Lords in Charles II's parliament and became a member of his privy council. He died at the age of eighty in 1662, and was buried, according to the DICTIONARY OF NATIONAL BIOGRAPHY, at Broughton, where he had lived for a time during the later Commonwealth period. The tradition, quoted by Chanter, that he died on Lundy and was buried under the west window of the chapel of St. Helen, is therefore incorrect.

In the year Old Subtlety died, a daughter was born to his son Nathaniel Fiennes, and was named Celia. On her 'Great Journey to Newcastle and Cornwall' in 1699 — published as THROUGH ENGLAND ON A SIDESADDLE in 1888 — Celia Fiennes rode from Camelford to Launceston. From there she claimed to have seen Hartland Point in the distance, 'and just by I saw the Isle of Lundy which formerly belonged to my grandfather William Lord Viscount Say and Seale which does abound with fish and rabbits and all sorts of fowls; one bird which lives partly in the water and partly out and so may be called an amphibious creature, its true one foote is like a turkey the other a gooses foote, it lays its eggs in a place the Sun shines on and sets it so exactly upright on the small end, and there it remains till taken up and all the art and skill of persons cannot set it up soe to abide . . . '.[10]

It is strange that such an experienced, though insular, traveller as Old Subtlety's granddaughter should have swallowed this tale of the diverse-footed fowl. By repeating it, one can only feel that, whatever her grandfather may have done, she has indeed 'writ a romance'.

Chapter Six

Although during the Commonwealth period French, Dutch and Spanish privateers still put to sea, Cromwell's navy seems to have prevented them from achieving much in British waters; it also blockaded foreign ports from which they sailed. Even licensed piracy by British ships was strictly controlled; few letters of marque were issued — in fact none at all after 1655.[1]

After the Restoration the old troubles resumed. In the late 1660s French pirates were preying on ships sailing to ports in Cornwall, Somerset and Devon. The Irish were exporting livestock in quantity; small barks carrying bullocks and sheep, as well as wool and tallow, were seized in 1667. In June of that year three French ships near Lundy 'put a terror into all vessels that were there, or that would come there'; much shooting had been heard for several days.

One French ship took a trow (trows were large flat-bottomed sailing barges much used on the Severn) and had the effrontery to hold the captain and put the crew ashore at Barnstaple to collect money to redeem the trow and her cargo — though they had taken a hundred sheep out of her, as well as provisions.[2]

This was the time of the Second Dutch War. In the previous year a Dutch fleet had sailed up the Medway and caused considerable damage; understandably, there was widespread alarm, an alarm which underlies a letter that appears among the State Papers warning that Lundy was 'very slenderly guarded . . . if the Dutch should take the island, it would block up the Severn, and a dozen good men could secure it from the world.' The writer was concerned that 'four or five men from a vessel riding on a cross wind' had been able to climb some gates (on the track up from the landing beach, presumably) and reach houses before the inhabitants realized they had landed.[3]

Grose, whose ANTIQUITIES were published in 1776, included a story about a horrible misuse of the islanders' hospitality that happened in the reign of William and Mary — in other words about eighty years before he was writing. A 'ship of force, pretending to be a Dutchman' sent a boat ashore to ask for milk for their sick captain. The milk was supplied for several days, until the captain was reported to have died, and the crew asked leave to bury him on the island, which was granted. All the islanders were asked to be present, but after a coffin had been carried into the church they were asked to leave for a few minutes. A short time later the door was flung open and the 'Dutchmen' — now revealed as Frenchmen — rushed out armed with weapons concealed in the 'coffin' and took them prisoner. 'They then seized 50 horses, 300 goats, 500 sheep, hamstrung the rest of the horses and bullocks, threw the goats and sheep into the sea and stripped the inhabitants of every valuable, even to their clothes, and spoiled and destroyed everything, and then, satiated with plunder and mischief, they threw the guns over the cliffs, and left the island in a most destitute and disconsolate condition.'

Chanter observes that there are strong grounds for disbelieving this sad story, as an almost identical one was told by Sir Walter Raleigh in his HISTORY OF THE WORLD; also the quantity of stock is improbably high. As a piece of senseless brutality it certainly appears questionable: to throw a total of 800 animals over the cliffs would have been a slow and exhausting business, and even in the twentieth century Lundy goats have never been easy to catch. Moreover, since the Frenchmen possessed arms, the cruel slow-motion hoax played on the islanders would have been unnecessary. Finally the reference to the church is puzzling. Only the little chapel of St. Helen's presumably existed — and that had been reported by Risdon as in ruins in the 1620s. The islanders would have needed to have done some substantial rebuilding since then to make it possible for the invaders to lock them out. However, the story finds acceptance by one modern writer. He suggests that the stratagem described by Raleigh was simply used again on a copycat principle. He also cites a report by the Bristol Society of Merchants in 1743 that during the wars with France of 1689-97 and 1702-13, 'French privateers possessed themselves, whenever they thought fit, of the island of Lundy.' He adds that some of the cannon said to have been thrown over the cliff were still to be seen at low tide during the 19th century. Even today, there is a place called Frenchman's Landing.[4]

Possibly the reality was a raid by Frenchmen, or a series of raids, their effects telescoped into a legend of one episode of savagery.

Smuggling was going on at the end of the 17th century, but the smugglers were English. A Richard Fulford applied to be made a Customs officer on Lundy, saying that considerable quantities of goods were run from there. The Commissioners of Customs told him that the island 'was hardly habited or habitable' — which was hardly the point, if it was only being used as a depot. In the 1720s a smuggler was living on the island; his name was Richard Scores, and he was probably a north Devon man. The Bristol merchants mentioned above as complaining about the French privateers thought that the island should be cultivated in order to maintain a garrison of about forty men 'with some few cannon and other military stores', who would protect trade in the Bristol Channel. The government only provided a sloop to patrol the seas between the Isles of Scilly and Lundy, but the Bristol merchants took things into their own hands and from then on protected their own vessels effectively.[5]

Until the 1740s Lundy apparently remained without any permanent inhabitants. It was then rented by the last man who would use it for illegal purposes, Thomas Benson.[6]

He was a Bideford merchant who could well have lived comfortably on the considerable fortune — said to have amounted to £40,000 — which he had inherited on the death of his elder brother. Such a life did not satisfy him; he would seem to have been one of those for whom accumulating money for its own sake, through risky ventures which gradually shade into lawless ones, satisfy something in their natures.

His legitimate business might have gone on making him rich: he imported tobacco from the American colonies and exported Barnstaple woollen goods in return; he owned a number of ships, including vessels that fished in Newfoundland waters; he was a coal merchant and manufactured rope. In addition he fitted out a merchant ship — naming her the *Benson Galley* — as a privateer, which took a number of valuable prizes before being captured by two French men-of-war during the time England was at war with France and Spain.

By 1746 Benson was sufficiently influential to be appointed Sheriff of Devon, and it was intimated to him that he might think of entering parliament. He presented the corporation of Barnstaple with a magnificent silver punchbowl, and at the next election was rewarded by being returned, with Henry Rolle, as MP for the borough. He took his seat in the parliament of 1747.

He had friends in high places, the foremost being Lord Gower, Lord Privy Seal (created Earl Gower in 1746). Lord Gower and his cousin Lord Carteret, formerly Secretary of State, were descendants of Sir Richard Grenville. Benson leased Lundy from them in 1748 for £60 a year. It had been uninhabited for nearly thirty years, since Richard Scores has been arrested for smuggling. Benson's noble landlords can hardly have suspected that he wanted the island for similar purposes.

His first idea was questionable though not actually illegal. He had obtained, probably through the good offices of Lord Gower, a contract to transport convicts — many of them likely to have been guilty of no more than petty theft — to Maryland, the colony with which he was already trading. Why, he reasoned, take up valuable cargo space in his ships on the long slow crossing of the Atlantic when the human freight could be landed much nearer at hand? He took them to Lundy, and used them to work at building walls and cultivating the land. When this ploy was discovered, he protested that he had never contracted to take the convicts to America, only out of England.

High excise duties on non-essentials such as wine, spirits, silk and tobacco made the 18th century the heyday of smuggling. Benson saw Lundy as an ideal depot for goods brought from abroad in his ships. Much of the contraband could be stored in a large man-made cavern at the south end of the island, still known as Benson's cave though probably cut out earlier, possibly during Bushell's occupation of the island.

Benson still lived at his boyhood home, Knapp House, on the hill above Appledore, which he had inherited as part of the family estate. No doubt he often entertained there people whom he wanted to impress, or who could be of use to him. In July, 1752, he arranged for several guests, including Sir Thomas Gunstone, Sheriff of Somerset, to pay a visit to Lundy 'in a little vessel bound for Wales, which dropped us in Lundy Road' — thus presumably thriftily combining hospitality and trade. Benson did not go with them; he was 'expecting letters from his insurance office for the vessel and cargo which was to have taken us there. The vessel lay off his quay with convicts bound for Virginia.' The barely seaworthy old ship, of seventy tons, was the *Nightingale*; the letters from the insurers were an important part of Benson's latest scheme.

He joined his guests two days later. The anonymous member of the party who left an account of the expedition says that the island's houses, built on either side of a platform, were miserably bad. When on the island Benson stayed in one, with any visitors, his servants in the other, but his convicts lived in the old fort — Bushell's Civil War fort, presumably — and were locked up every night when they had finished their work. Shortly before the narrator's party arrived, seven or eight of them managed to take a long boat, escape to Hartland and disappear.

Benson sounds a frugal host: 'Had it not been for the supply of rabbits and young seagulls our table would have been but poorly furnished, rats being so plenty that they destroyed every night what we left of our repast by day. Lobsters were tolerably plentiful, and some fish we caught.' The 'cave or magazine where Mr. Benson lodged his goods' is mentioned; steps cut in the rock led up to it, with a rope to help climbers.

Only a few days after his guests had retired to the mainland — eager for a square meal, perhaps — Benson gave orders for the *Nightingale* to sail. She was laden with cutlery, pewter, woollen goods, lace and silk — and the convicts. John Lancey, a young seaman who had worked for Benson for some time, had been persuaded to agree to his master's plan for disposing of the ship. He landed the goods on Lundy, sailed some distance from the island and set fire to the *Nightingale*, carefully following Benson's instructions. The convicts and crew were rescued by another ship and put ashore at Clovelly. The operation might have succeeded, if one of the crew had not got drunk and told a Barnstaple merchant — an enemy of Benson's — exactly what had happened aboard the *Nightingale*.

That a prosperous and successful merchant, an MP with friends among the nobility and gentry, should have indulged first in smuggling and then in a somewhat crude insurance swindle, seems hardly comprehensible — unless his behaviour in front of his guests on Lundy (to whom, incidentally, he freely admitted his double dealing in the matter of transporting convicts) may be seen as an indication of a somewhat irrational state of mind.

The narrator already quoted observed 'There happened to come into the roads one evening near twenty sail of vessels. The colours were hoisted on the fort, and they all as they passed Rat island returned the compliment except one vessel, which provoked Mr. Benson to fire at her with ball, though we used every argument in our power to prevent him. He replied that the Island was his, and every vessel that passed it and did not pay him the same compliment as was paid to the king's forts he would fire at her.'

To begin with, the island was not his; he was only the tenant, and he certainly was not entitled to endanger life on passing ships by firing on them. His action suggests that he was beginning to indulge in delusions of grandeur and a defiant arrogance similar to those exhibited by the Mariscos and some of the later pirates who seized Lundy. In his dishonesties, it is as though he felt that he was above the law, or could flout it with impunity.

Yet with regard to the insurance money he hoped to obtain, there may have been a practical consideration. Rich man though he was, or had been, very heavy fines had been levied against him for omitting to pay duty on several cargoes of tobacco he had brought into Barnstaple since 1749. These might have crippled him financially, had he paid them. So far he had managed to avoid doing so, but he must have known that he could not delay much longer. Moreover he would almost certainly have known that Customs officers were becoming suspicious that he was using Lundy as a base for smuggling.

In 1753 new fines were added to those he already owed. His estate, including Knapp House, was confiscated. It became clear that when John Lancey and other members of the crew came to trial they would be found guilty (as indeed they were, and the unfortunate Lancey was sentenced to death) and he himself would be held responsible. He fled to Portugal, where he managed to build up a trading company again. He died in Oporto at the age of 64.

John Lancey was hanged at Execution Dock in June, 1754. Lord Gower died in the same year; not long before his death a contributor to the 'Gentleman's Magazine' wrote an account of Lundy which was published the following year.[7] He had heard that access was only possible in one place, 'and the avenue there is so narrow, that a few men might defend the pass against a multitude. If to this natural fortification a small fort had been added, the petty French privateers who lurked there in Queen Anne's war, to our great loss, might have been driven away. They took so many of our vessels, for which they lay in wait in this place, that they called it the Golden Bay. But tho' no fort is yet built, yet the Bristol privateers so effectively protected the trade in this place, during the last war (i.e. the war against Spain and France, which was largely a maritime conflict) that not a single vessel was taken.'

It sounds as though the writer had no personal knowledge of Lundy, since he seems unaware that there was a fort of sorts — the one in which Benson locked up his convicts — and he makes no mention of Benson. However, the building was probably of little defensive use by the time he was writing.

During the next two decades no one appeared willing to take possession of the island, let alone fortify it. One family remained there for a time; according to the 'Gentleman's Magazine' they lived by selling liquor to passing fishermen, which sounds a precarious trade. Once they had left, the island remained uninhabited until it was bought by a rich young Cambridge graduate, John Borlase Warren, who wanted it originally as an anchorage for his yacht. His ownership put an end to the seven centuries of intermittent violence and lawlessness. He was able to sail his yacht in the seas around the island without fear of attack by pirates, and the new inhabitants he encouraged to settle had no need to keep watch for raiders. Moreover he was not simply interested in sailing. He may be seen as virtually the first owner who did not want the island for what he could get out of it. On the contrary, he spent a great deal of money in a short time in an attempt to reclaim it for agriculture, establishing several farms.

It was perhaps a thankless task, as well as an expensive one. After only six years he exchanged yachting for more serious seamanship: he served in the war of American Independence as a naval officer, finally becoming Admiral of the White and an ambassador.[8] However, he left a foundation on which his successors could build.

GUILLEMOT AND GANNET.

Chapter Seven

Three accounts of Lundy have survived from the last quarter of the 18th century, two of them written in 1775, the year Warren bought the island for only £510. One is included in Francis Grose's ANTIQUITIES OF ENGLAND AND WALES; it gives details of the island's mostly ruinous buildings, in particular the castle, and contains references to the various springs that supplied inhabitants with water. The other, by the Rev. Thomas Martyn, who had been Warren's tutor, was used in evidence 'in the course of Chancery proceedings in 1776', according to Chanter, who adds that it must be taken with some reserve, as 'he appears to have gone there as an interested witness purposely to depreciate the value in order to help his former pupil's case.'

Martyn spent about ten days on the island in September, 1775. Warren had already begun an attempt to make improvements by planting trees, but without avail: they were all withered and dead. About 500 acres at the south end, Martyn suggested, might support lean Welsh cattle, but all the rest was 'incorrigibly barren', overrun by rats and rabbits. Where there was any soil it was shallow and poor; elsewhere the rocks were covered only by heath and moss. The only possible use for the place was as pasture for store cattle, though the expense of transporting them to and from the mainland might render this unprofitable.

However grateful Warren may have been for Martyn's pessimistic view of Lundy (he later presented him to the living of Little Marlow, of which he was the patron) he probably discounted it from the beginning, and once secure in ownership, went ahead with plans to bring the island back into cultivation, as a 'Journal of the time we spent on the Island of Lundy, July, 1787' indicates. The anonymous diarist, referred to simply as 'a gentleman', had also written the account of the visit in 1752, in Benson's time, already quoted. His observations survive because in the early 1820s a group of amateur *literati* in Barnstaple formed what they called the Cavern Club, and produced a magazine to which they contributed 'a miscellaneous collection of original prose and poetry, reviewing and riddles' as the first editor put it. Circulated originally in manuscript, it appeared in printed form in January, 1824, as 'The Cave and Lundy Review, or Critical Revolving Light' (the revolving light being that of Lundy's first lighthouse, built only a few years earlier). Under this title it lasted for six issues; after a month's break it then emerged as 'The North Devon Magazine', with the same contributors, and finally folded in April, 1825.

The 'Journals' of 1752 and 1787 appeared in the first number of the 'The Cave and Lundy Review'. The 1787 diary begins: 'I sailed from Appledore in the *Viper* sloop-of-war, July 4th, 1787, commanded by Lieut. Chrymes, with Captain Barton, Messrs Cleveland, Roberts and Thomas Cutcliffe, and the Rev. Mr. Smith of Westleigh'. They weighed anchor at 8.00 a.m. and did not reach the island until 3.00 p.m., which suggests that they had to tack against contrary winds. Just how the party had arranged for themselves to be transported aboard HMS *Viper* is not explained. Cleveland, mentioned as one of the party, was John Cleveland, owner of Tapeley (then spelled Tapley) Park, Instow and also, by this time, owner of Lundy. He was one of Barnstaple's two MPs (having been first elected in 1766 he was to serve in seven successive parliaments, ending in 1796). It must be assumed that he had considerable local influence, and Lieut. Chrymes and other officers may have enjoyed his hospitality.

The diarist mentions Sir John Warren several times. In a note he remarks that Sir John began a quay 'which was never finished, though the materials were exceedingly good for the purpose, being large moorstones, of which there was a great plenty on the island, and might be converted to great profit by skilful persons.' The party 'went to the house which Sir John Warren built for his own purpose', and after dinner 'on a pleasant spot between the chapel and the house . . . saw the ground Sir John had marked out to build a handsome house on.'

A distinction is made between the Castle, entirely demolished, on 'the extremity of the south part of the island, facing Hartland Point' on two acres of ground, surrounded by stone walls and ditch (in other words Bushell's Civil War fort, later used by Benson for his convicts) from what is called the Citadel — Henry III's castle — the walls of which were 'very perfect, of a square form; it is converted into modern dwellings, the turrets which were chimneys still serve the same purpose of which there are four — one at each angle. The south-west wall is nearly 51 feet, the north-west $38^1/_2$. In front of the house five guns are planted. The garrison was supplied with water from a spring which rises above the house built by Sir John Warren; it was conveyed from thence in earthenware pipes, some of which I brought home with me.' Once again the cave used by Benson is mentioned.

The party amused themselves in typical 18th century fashion by aimlessly shooting at seabirds. They also tried to row round the island (a brisk gale sprang up and drove them back) and went fishing.

Like the inhabitants of some other islands around the coasts of Britain, the people of Lundy slaughtered enormous numbers of seabirds, catching them in nets similar to those used for rabbits, which they fixed on sticks at breeding places. 'Every morning and evening the natives watch their nets, and take out the birds that are caught. They catch in a good season 1,700 or 1,800 dozen, and make a shilling a pound of their feathers. People from the neighbouring coast are hired to pluck them, at twopence a dozen, and pluck four dozen a day.' Twelve birds produced a pound of feathers; after being plucked they were skinned, and the skins were boiled in a furnace for the oil they yielded, which was used for lighting. Finally the flesh was given to the pigs, 'which feed on it voraciously.' This may account for the fact that a note was added to the list of stock on the island that 'The flesh of the hogs bred on the island cannot be eat;

the flesh is yellow and strong.' There were thirty of them, as well as thirty bullocks, twenty cows, seven sheep, seven horses, sixteen deer and seven goats.

Not only did the islanders destroy such numbers of birds that it seems extraordinary that any colonies were left, (1,700 or 1,800 dozen is, after all, more than 20,000), but they collected their eggs, which were sent to Bristol sugar refineries, though for what purpose is not explained. This way of earning a living was apparently preferred to actual farming; the people 'sowed but small crops, trusting to their birds and rabbits to pay their rent' — which was seventy pounds a year. Rabbits lived mostly on the western side; the islanders caught 'about 1,000 couple' a year, eating the meat and selling the skins.

Sir John Warren had let the island on 21 year leases, which Cleveland was presumably continuing. Having completed the second of the walls begun by Benson's convict labour (now known as the Halfway Wall) he had enclosed about 160 acres, dividing them into fields of seven, eight or ten acres in which barley, oats and, it was said, wheat were grown. Unhappily, the tenants frequently disagreed among themselves; one of Cleveland's reasons for visiting the island was to try to settle their disputes, as well as swearing in one of the farmers, a Mr. Hole, as constable, to see they kept the peace. (The following year Mr. Hole, collecting seabirds' eggs, fell over a cliff and was killed).

The diarist took part in Cleveland's discussions. He may well have been a Bideford lawyer, and have been one of the 1752 party also because he was an adviser to Benson.

On July 8th, Sunday, 'the Rev. Cutcliffe read prayers and Mr. Smith preached a sermon to 22 persons.' The diarist does not say where this service was held, but it has been conjectured that it was in the ruins of the ancient chapel dedicated to St. Helen. The party had visited it on the day of their arrival. It was on the highest part of the island: 'some of the walls remained; the entrance, built of moorstone or spar, was from the north; its length about 25 feet, breadth 12 feet, doorway 4 feet, thickness of walls nearly $2^1/_2$ feet.' There are several historic references to a chapel of St. Anne on Lundy, and there have been various theories about its position and identity: Chanter suggests that it was an oratory attached to St. Helen's. The latter first appears in ecclesiastical records as early as 1254, when Adam de Aston was placed by mandate in possession of the church on 'Lunday'. It is referred to in fact as the church of St. Mary, but this may be an error on the part of a medieval clerk. Between that date and 1384 six priests were appointed; from then until the time of the suppression of the monasteries, when Cleeve Abbey, in Somerset, had the patronage of the rectory of Lundy, nothing is known of any priest who may have ministered to the little chapel.[1]

After a night of thick heavy rain and strong wind, the diarist again spent some time hearing the islanders' complaints, after which he borrowed a horse and rode to the north end of the island, where he saw the result of Benson's decision to set the bracken and heather on fire some 35 years earlier: it had burned for some days, until it came to bare rock; no vegetation remained. He saw deer and goats, which ran for cover in the high bracken of the cleaves. Mr. Hole showed him the old batteries on the rocks. Meanwhile the Rev. Smith and Captain Barton had been out with their guns. The former shot a doe, but 'she proved but thin meat'. In fact provisions were running low, as on the 1752 visit, and the party decided to leave the next day. Accordingly they got up at four a.m., packed up their bedding and sailed at eight, 'leaving all the inhabitants in seeming good humour with each other.'

One more description of the island as it was during Cleveland's ownership may be found in the fourth volume of THE BEAUTIES OF ENGLAND AND WALES, by E. Brayley and J. Britton, published in 1803. By that time there were said to be 400 acres in cultivation, 300 arable and the rest pasture; there were 400 sheep, 80 cattle and 12 deer, as well as a quantity of pigs and poultry. Wheat was the principal produce, while potatoes and turnips were good. This suggests that Cleveland had managed to dissuade his tenant farmers from destroying the unfortunate guillemots, puffins and gannets in such huge numbers, and stealing their eggs, in order to

Plate 4

The Old Light

concentrate their energies rather more on agriculture.

He sold the island in 1803 to Sir Vere Hunt, a baronet from Curragh, Limerick, for £700. In one of the copies of Chanter's monograph in the North Devon Athenaeum, Barnstaple, there is a cutting from an unnamed and undated newspaper, probably of the 19th century. It describes the sale. 'It was Mr. Aubrey de Vere's grandfather who bought Lundy Island, in the Bristol Channel, by accident. Once, when walking in a London street, he passed a room where an auction was going on, and, attracted by the noise, entered it. The property set up for auction was Lundy Island. He knew nothing whatever about it, but when the auctioneer proclaimed it had never paid either tax or tithe, that it acknowledged neither King nor Parliament, nor law civil or ecclesiastical, and that its proprietor was Pope and Emperor at once in his own scanty domain, he made a bid, and it was knocked down to him. It turned out to be a good speculation. It paid its cost by the sale of rabbits, and whenever its purchaser chanced to have a quarrel with England and Ireland at the same time, it was a hermitage to which he could always retire and meditate. He planted there a small Irish colony, and drew up for them a compendious code, including a quaint law of divorce in case of matrimonial disputes. In money matters he was adventurous and unlucky. He lost about £15,000 at cards, and then renounced them. He is said to have lost about half the family property through some trivial offence given to his father.'

What became of Cleveland's tenants does not appear. In 1794 there were said to be seven houses and 23 inhabitants.[2] By about 1836 there was one farmhouse (the one that had been repaired by Sir John Warren) which was 'the only residence except a cottage for the accommodation of the Trinity Company, 'Johnny Groat's house', a small cottage at the north point, and two residences for workmen.'[2] Perhaps Hunt had ended the farm leases, and compelled their occupants to return to the mainland. According to L. R. W. Loyd, the Irish colonists did much damage 'and their destructive habits continued until the island was sold in 1830'.[3] Although Loyd says that it was Sir Aubrey de Vere Hunt, who inherited the island on his father's death in 1818, who brought the Irish to the island, the cutting quoted above indicates that this was incorrect.)

The large numbers of wrecks on the island and in the approaches to the Bristol Channel had aroused calls for a lighthouse for many years. During Cleveland's ownership merchants of Bristol had offered to build one at their own expense; one of the objects of the 1787 visit was to meet some of them to decide on the best site. Although Beacon Hill was chosen, no building followed.

However, Trinity House eventually decided that a light must be built, and obtained a lease of land on Beacon Hill for 999 years, beginning on 1st July, 1819. It is, in Pevsner;'s words, 'a beautifully proportioned structure 90 feet high'.[4] Chanter gives details: 'The lights as seen from the sea are two: the westerly light, which is seen by vessels coming up Channel, in a broad, steady beam of light, and is useful to vessels as a warning they are getting too near the shore, as it then disappears, being shut out by the intermediate summit of the cliffs. The other and main light is a revolving lantern on the top . . . it sends out streams of brilliant flashes visible every two minutes.' Half a mile to the north a battery of two eighteen-pounders fired a round every ten minutes in foggy weather.

Unfortunately no one had considered a special feature of Lundy's climate: the tendency for thick mists to gather on the tableland around Beacon Hill, even when at a lower level there might be fair visibility. The light was thus often obscured. For the greater part of the 19th century, therefore, until the present north and south lights were built, shipping found the earlier lighthouse only intermittently useful.

In 1830 Sir Aubrey Hunt sold Lundy for £4,500 - a striking increase in value compared with the price his grandfather had paid 27 years earlier. The joint buyers were John Matravers, one of William IV's Gentlemen-at-Arms, and a Somerset man, William Stiffe. Four years later they put it on the market again. In 1836 there began an entirely new regime for Lundy under the ownership of William Hudson Heaven and, later, his son.

Chapter Eight

William Hudson Heaven inherited money from a godfather who owned sugar plantations in Jamaica.[1] When slaves were emancipated in 1834, estate owners were given compensation. The large sum Heaven received made it possible for him to pay £9,870 to Matravers and Stiffe, who thus made a profit of rather more than a hundred per cent on their outlay in 1830.

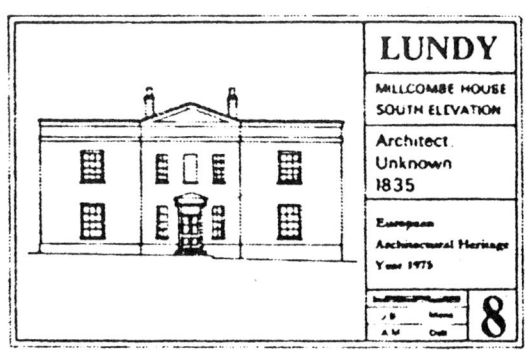

Having built a house (known to the Heaven family as The Villa, but later called Millcombe) and a new road leading up from the landing beach, Heaven seems to have considered the expense of running the island, in addition to his house in Somerset, as too great, and put it on the market. Although it did not find a buyer, the farm was let.

During the next decade, the Heaven family spent their summers on Lundy, returning to their home on the mainland each autumn. William's wife Cecilia, having borne ten children, and lost four of them in infancy, in about eighteen years, died in 1851 at the age of 47. From then on William Heaven spent the greater part of his time on Lundy as the benevolent patriarch of the sort of large, extended family that was so characteristic of the Victorian age.

Born in Bristol in 1799, he was educated at Harrow and Exeter College, Oxford, made the conventional Grand Tour and at the age of 26 married Cecilia Grosett, the daughter of a Rear-Admiral. Sustained by an income from the Jamaican plantations, he never had to consider earning a living. He was said to be 'full of fun, generous and kindly, with a keen sense of humour'. A Tory, he kept 'bits of landed property to give him the right to vote'. He was, it seems, an autocrat. Bearing in mind that the island had been a medieval Manor, he liked always to be known as the Squire; Kelly's Directory of 1883 refers to him as 'lord of the manor (which retains very full manorial rights) and sole landowner.' Moreover he was unwilling to admit that Lundy was not an independent domain, outside the jurisdiction of mainland authority. He refused to allow a small school he set up for the island children to be inspected; he refused to complete census forms; he refused to allow police to land on the island in 1871 to arrest a man accused of murder after an affray, although he did ensure that the man was shipped to the mainland to be taken into custody; his son, the Rev. Heaven, gave evidence at the coroner's inquest in Ilfracombe. (The man was acquitted and discharged.)

He set up on the landing beach a concrete block enclosing a slab of slate on which was inscribed 'This island is private. There are no public roads, footpaths or rights of ways (sic) whatever hereon.'[2] According to Felix Gade, 'this had been erected by an irate Mr. W.H. Heaven as an answer to the impudence of Trinity House in having erected a granite stone on which there were the initials TH 1819, signifying the year in which the Brethren first landed on Lundy for the purpose of building a lighthouse'. Just what was impudent about Trinity House setting up their stone is hard to see, especially as they had presumably done so about seventeen years before Heaven bought the island. Both marker stones were destroyed in a landslide in November, 1954.[3]

Though he might have thought it presumptuous to call himself King of Lundy, as the pirate Thomas Salkeld had done, under Heaven's ownership the island almost inevitably came to be known as the Kingdom of Heaven, a joke repeated tirelessly throughout the second half of the 19th century and into the 20th.

His eldest son, Hudson, obtained a third in Lit. Hum. at Trinity College, Oxford, at the age of 25, in 1851. Having converted the degree to an M.A. in the following year, he became a deacon, and was ordained priest in 1854. He spent two years on the staff of Ilminster Grammar School before becoming first an assistant master at Taunton Collegiate School and then headmaster from 1858-64. The school failed, and he returned to Lundy, where he was licenced curate-in-charge until 1886. Thereafter, having built the church of St. Helena on the island, he was its vicar.[4]

He did not marry, and was said to be of a retiring and studious disposition; in the family, his nickname was Phi, short for philosopher.

His younger brothers were more adventurous — necessarily, as money was lacking to give them a university education. Walter Hope Heaven, born in 1829, emigrated to Australia and married there. Three years after his death at the age of 36 his wife Marion was welcomed as a part of the family group on Lundy, with her two young children, Walter and Winnie. The third son, de Boniot Spencer Heaven, also went abroad; having worked for some time for the P and O Company, he spent the greater part of his later life in Jamaica, managing the plantations his father had inherited.

When their mother died her three surviving daughters, Cecilia, Amelia and Lucy, were 20, 18 and 15 respectively. Their life from then on was doubly restricted: by the conventions of the Victorian middle class and by their isolation. The approved escape route was of course marriage, but here again there could have been snags — not merely the fact of living on a remote island, but their father's possessiveness. His granddaughter recorded that he was 'passionately fond of his daughters and it was said he promptly pitched his tent elsewhere when a suitor came on the scene, for fear of losing them'. In spite of this Cecilia became engaged when she was acting as housekeeper at her brother's school in Taunton. The engagement was a long one; Cecilia returned to Lundy when the school closed, and in 1865 her health began to fail. She died in 1879, still unmarried, at the age of 48. Amelia was said to have received 36 proposals of marriage, yet to have been unwilling to leave Lundy for any of her suitors. Or can it have been that her father's anxiety to retain her company dissuaded her?

The girls, their widowed sister-in-law, and any visiting female cousins and aunts, occupied their days in ways approved for leisured women of their period: they walked and read, tended the garden, embroidered, sketched and wrote letters, played cards or games, taught the children of their tiny village, and visited the sick when necessary. Amelia almost certainly helped to entertain them with music: she was said to be a brilliant pianist, as well as a good artist and linguist. There were holidays on the mainland or abroad. An unfortunate visit to London in 1862 resulted in the death of Lucy, of typhoid, at the age of 24.

Casual visitors who might arrive by boat were welcomed, providing they belonged to the stratum of society that observed the convention of presenting visiting cards. Such cards would be scrutinized at The Villa, and their owners might be invited for refreshments, and conducted on a tour of the island.

However, one visitor who arrived on an August day in 1849 does not seem to have made any attempt to meet the Heaven family. He was Charles Kingsley, thirty years old, exhausted by his parish work at Eversley and by money worries, the latter caused largely by his wife's extravagance. He had spent the early part of the year in Ilfracombe, with his family; now on his doctor's advice he had come back for another rest, alone, staying in lodgings in Clovelly, the village he knew so well from his boyhood, when his father had been vicar of the parish.

He joined a group organized by his landlady and her husband: 'Some dozen young men and women, sons and daughters of the wealthier coasting captains and owners of fishing smacks'. In a cutter with red sails they left Clovelly pier at six in the morning; the crossing took five hours. (In those days it could take considerably longer if the wind was adverse.) Once they were under way, an older woman whom Kingley calls the Wesleyan abbess of the town, 'with her tall, slim, queenly figure, massive forehead, wild glittering eyes, features beaming with tenderness and enthusiasm' took out a Wesleyan hymn book and 'gave out the Morning Hymn, apparently as a matter of course'. Her fellow passengers made it a musical voyage: ' . . . one sweet voice after another arose; then a man gained courage, and chimed in with a full harmonious bass: then a rich sad alto made itself heard, as it wandered in and out between the voices of the men and women; and at last a wild mellow tenor, which we discovered, after much searching, to proceed from the unlikely-looking lips of an old, dry, weather-bleared, mummified chrysalis of a man, who stood aft, steering with his legs . . .'[5]

In a letter to his wife Kingsley said, 'I saw the old Pirate Moresco's (sic) Castle on the cliff — the awful granite cliffs on the west, with their peaks and chasms lined with sea fowl — the colouring wonderful — pink and grey granite, with bright yellow lichen spots, purple heather, and fern of a peculiar dark glowing green. You wanted no trees; the beauty of their rich forms and simple green was quite replaced by the gorgeous brilliance of the hues. And beyond and around all, the illimitable Atlantic — not green — but an intense sapphirine black-hue, such as it never is inshore; and so clear, that every rock and patch of sea-weed showed plain four hundred feet below us, through the purple veil of water. Then I went back to the landing cove, where shoals of mackeral were breaking up with a roar, like the voice of many waters; the cove like glass; and one huge seal rolling his black head and shoulders about in the water — a sight to remember for ever. (In a published essay he said a man on the boat shot the seal.) Oh, that I had been a painter, for that day at least! And coming away, as the sun set behind the island, great flame-coloured sheets of rack flared up into the black sky from off the black line of the island top; and when the sun set the hymns began again, and we slipped on home, while every ripple of the cutter's bow fell down, and ran along the surface in flakes and sparkles of emerald fire . . . '

The wind fell light, and the cutter ghosted back to the harbour of Clovelly at two o'clock in the morning.

Five years later Kingsley would spend six months in Bideford, and in that half-year, from June to December, would write the long novel that would set him free of money worries for the rest of his life: WESTWARD HO! The climax of that remarkable Elizabethan romance is well known: the great storm in which Amyas Leigh pursues the Armada ship, Don Guzman's *Santa Catharina*, around Land's End and northwards until he suddenly recognizes that the dark bank ahead is the south end of Lundy, with the Shutter rock, 'like a huge black fang' on which the *Santa Catharina* impales herself. The English seamen fall silent as they watch the galleon 'heel over from the wind, and sweep headlong down the cataract of the race, plunging her yards into the foam, and showing her whole black side even to her keel, until she rolled clean over, and vanished for ever and ever'.

Balked of his wish to kill Don Guzman, his rival for the love of Rose Salterne as well as his enemy in war, in personal combat, Amyas hurls his sword into the sea in fury — and at the same moment is struck blind by a tremendous lightning flash.

This is not, however, the only mention of Lundy in the novel. Kingsley presumably felt that there was a form of poetic justice in the fact that the *Santa Catharina* was wrecked on the island, because it was there that Don Guzman took Rose on the first stage of their voyage to Caracas when he persuaded her to run away with him; they sheltered in the Marisco Castle. The unfortunate tenant, John Braund, is later arrested, taken to Exeter and imprisoned on a charge of 'harbouring priests, Jesuits, Gipsies and other suspect and traitorous, persons'. He dies soon afterwards of gaol fever.

Any visitor who wanted to stay on Lundy in the mid-19th century but was not a friend or relation of William Heaven could be put up at the farm. A naturalist who arrived three years after Kingsley reported that he found the accommodation 'decent (for the circumstances), a well-supplied table, attendance prompt and kindly, and charge moderate'. He also describes the farmer, John Lee (an ex-seaman always known as Captain Jack) who had by that time been William Heaven's tenant for some ten years, as 'an excellent, worthy man' — though the Heaven family were later to accuse him of smuggling and non-payment of rent, and end his tenancy.

The visiting naturalist was Philip Gosse. Like Kingsley, he had been advised by his doctor to spend a holiday in the country for the sake of his health. He had chosen south Devon first, but after two months decided that it was not bracing enough, and moved, with his wife and small son, to Ilfracombe.[6] The result of his stay would be a book published in 1853, A NATURALIST'S RAMBLES ON THE

Plate 5

William Hudson Heaven

DEVONSHIRE COAST. He also wrote a series of articles for a magazine, the 'Home Friend', published weekly for the S.P.C.K. at one penny and described as 'A weekly miscellany of Amusement and Instruction'. They later appeared in book form under the title SEA AND LAND.

In the first article he spoke of often gazing out upon Lundy 'from the lofty cliffs and downs around Ilfracombe', and wishing to explore it. His wish was granted 'through the courtesy of Hudson Heaven, Esq., the eldest son of the proprietor, who kindly invited myself and two companions to accompany him on his boat . . . ' With 'portmanteau and carpet-bags, collecting basket, bottles and jars for zoophytes' they set sail on a cold July morning. A heavy sea was running and soon the passengers, soaked by a huge wave breaking over the boat, were chilled and seasick. They had to endure a voyage of eight hours. As they drew near the island Mr. Heaven 'pointed out different objects of interest, and gave us legendary and statistical information'. About twenty vessels were lying at anchor, of various sizes from 'stately three-masted ship to tiny fishing skiff'. That was nothing, Mr. Heaven told them; he had seen as many as three hundred sheltering in the roadstead.

Gosse was not only a marine biologist (he called himself a littoral naturalist) but a botanist, and on the way up from the landing beach he noted twenty different wild flowers, from mallow and stonecrop to foxglove and honeysuckle; during his stay on the island he was to delight in recognising many more.

After a meal at the farmhouse, he and his companions went out to explore the south end and the Marisco Castle, where labourers' cottages had been built inside the walls by William Heaven. The sight of small children running and jumping on the edge of the precipice made the visitors shudder, but when they spoke to a woman about the danger, she seemed not to understand what they were talking about. 'Great mixens outside the doors, strewn with the shells of enormous limpets, and with those of the green conical eggs of guillemots, afforded amusing evidence of the favourite food of the poorer inhabitants of the island'. (Did the use of the word 'amusing' in such a context jar on any reader of 'Home Friend'?)

On a walk across the island Gosse noted large numbers of cocoons of burnet hawk moths. He evidently had a keen sense of hearing; having taken a few cocoons back to his bedroom at the farm, he heard faint creaking sounds coming from some of them at night. When he held them to the light the semi-transparency of the cocoons made it possible to see 'the enclosed pupa busily engaged in revolving on its long axis, and the sound was caused by the grating of its rings against the papery walls of its prison'.

Beyond the Halfway Wall he was attracted by the naturally occurring white quartz gravel on the paths and open ground, and was told that an attempt had been made to use it for garden walks 'but the absolute lack of any adhesive principle caused them to be rejected on trial . . . they would not *bind*'.

From the Templar rock he looked back and saw an example of that peculiarity of Lundy which had made the lighthouse of only limited use since it was built: its top was 'enveloped in a semi-transparent haze, that streamed off some distance to leeward like a white veil. We were informed that it is a common thing for the fog to lie on the heights of the island, while the sides, the beach, and the sea, are perfectly free from cloud . . . '

Beyond the Constable rock he and his companions came upon 'the scene which had been the chief object of our curiosity', the huge colonies of puffins and razorbills then to be seen at the north end of the island. Several varieties of gull were prudently 'wary and alert; we do not see them sitting still as we approach, as the puffins and razorbills do, for before we can get within gun range they are on the wing'.

One of the party 'knocked over a puffin with a clod of earth, just to examine it'. Having admired the stunned bird's plumage, they 'laid it on a rock in the sun, where no doubt it soon recovered'. Hudson Heaven, usually referred to as 'our friend', assured them that he himself has knocked down six with one stone (for what purpose he does not say) and that he had seen 'twenty-seven bagged from a single shot with an ordinary fowling piece, not reckoning many more which were knocked over, partially wounded, but which managed to fly out to sea'. The men who carried out this casual, aimless cruelty no doubt called themselves sportsmen. (Even Kingsley, in his essay already quoted, remarked in passing that 'We had shot along the cliffs a red-legged chough or two'.)

Yet Gosse and his friends were pleased to see a dozen or more gannets which, after 'being annoyed by idle gunners from the main', had almost deserted the island until recently.

It seems that puffins were still being caught for their feathers, although Chanter was to write that 'since the present owner's occupation neither birds nor their eggs or feathers have been a source of revenue'. The visitors saw tall iron rods which they were told were used to support a long narrow net that could be 'stretched along like a wall to intercept the puffins' as they flew from their nests.

From the furthest north-west point, where the North Light would be built nearly 50 years later, they looked down into 'the entrance of a fine cavern, sixty feet in height, about thirty in width, and perhaps eight hundred in length. It completely perforates a projecting promontory, the part of the coast, indeed, which we had been skirting'. Presumably Hudson Heaven provided these measurement; Chanter also says the tunnel is sixty feet high and about eight hundred long. Yet J. L. W. Page, writing in 1895, say that he rowed right through it, and it is about thirty feet high and 'at the outside, two hundred feet, probably not so much; certainly not more than a quarter of the length given by Mr. Chanter'.[7]

The cliff ledges at this extreme end of the island were crowded with guillemots; they watched parent birds bringing back beak-fulls of sand eels for their young and 'were at a loss to understand how the first capture could be retained in the beak in this orderly manner, or, indeed, held at all, while another was seized'. One of the party, having his fowling-piece handy, promptly shot a guillemot, and scientific curiosity was satisfied by an examination of the dead bird's beak. Guillemot's eggs were still being taken by youths on the island, as well as by visiting fishermen. 'In the season we see them offered for sale by these fishermen's children at Ilfracombe, at a penny each; and they may be purchased as curiosities by visitors, who are struck by their singularity and beauty'.

(And in fact the taking of eggs would go on into the twentieth century. In June, 1909, for instance, the remarkable young Barnstaple-born naturalist, Bruce Frederick Cummings who, as W.N.P. Barbellion, would publish his JOURNAL OF A DIS-APPOINTED MAN shortly before his early death, visited Lundy and stayed at the farmhouse. One evening the farmer's son occupied himself blowing 'seagulls' eggs'— species not specified — with his father's approval. The next day, Cummings recorded 'Out egg-collecting with the Lighthouse Keepers. They walk about the cliffs as sure footed as cats, and feed their dogs on birds' eggs collected in a little bag at the end of a long pole. One dog ate three right off in as many minutes, putting his teeth through and cracking the shell, then lapping up the contents'.)

Hudson Heaven evidently did all he could to ensure that Gosse and his companions explored the island as fully as possible during their stay. He guided them to the Devil's Limekiln along 'a broad road, marked off by stone posts at regular intervals, each bearing conspicuously painted the letters T.H.' — the road to the lighthouse on Beacon Hill. Gosse noted sheep's bit, samphire, cat's ear and stone-crop growing around the edges of the chasm, and when a bird flew out identified it as a kestrel. Like many visitors before and since, he was told that it was believed that if the Shutter rock could be lifted, turned over and dropped into the Devil's Limekiln, it would fit exactly.

With the help of Captain Jack Lee and his son, Captain Tom, and two ladders they scrambled down to Seal Cave, all getting a ducking from the waves surging over the approach to a rock at the cave mouth. They were warned that when they reached the narrowest part, a startled seal might rush out and knock them over. However, 'one of the servants, a cool resolute fellow, used to the warfare,' went ahead grasping a bludgeon. Fortunately for the unwarlike seals, there were none in the cavern that day. (Chanter speaks of 'sportsmen' who visited Lundy to prove their bravery by killing seals as they tried to flee in terror from the lights held by the invaders of their dark hiding place.)

After exploring the cave Gosse examined rock pools. The southwestern end of the island is slate, and he noted 'unusually fine' growths of dulse, carrageen moss, oarweeds and sea-thongs, as well as sea anemones, but saw no marine creatures to interest him.

The next day Tom Lee took them lobster fishing. Gosse called him 'a worthy fellow', kind-hearted and obliging, 'one that has read a good deal, and has seen something of the world'. Having recently lost his ship off the coast of Africa, Captain Tom had come back to Lundy to be a fisherman. (It may be assumed that it was another member of the family who appears in an entry in Billings' Directory of 1857: 'A vessel leaves Clovelly for the island (Lundy), under the command of Captain Robert Lee, once a fortnight during the winter months, and once a week and sometimes oftener during the summer'.)

Captain Tom rowed the visitors along the east side of the island to Gannet's Rock, where the Admiralty were thinking of making a harbour of refuge by building a breakwater (a plan that was considered by a Royal Commission a few years later, and approved, but eventually rejected as too expensive). He had sunk some thirty lobster pots; when these were hauled up they were found to have caught not only lobsters but crayfish, common crabs and spider crabs. For Gosse, the interest of the latter was to find them 'studded more or less densely with zoophytes of the genera *Sertularia, Plumularia*, etc., sponges and seaweed'.

Although thunder showers had drenched everyone in the boat, it was decided to dredge for oysters before going ashore. 'On the eastern side of the island the proprietor, some years since, had endeavoured to form an oyster bed; the ground was suitable, and he had stocked up with living oysters. The result of the experiment had not yet been tested, and it was proposed that we should make the first examination'.

It was not promising: three hauls only brought up a few oysters. Again it was the forms of marine life to be found on the shells that attracted Gosse; he made a drawing of one, a plant-like polyp, *Plumularia Catharina*. He collected a number of zoophytes to take back to Ilfracombe to be studied at leisure, and declared the day to have been one of 'much gratification', despite the weather. 'The disagreeables were nothing, or at least they lost their disagreeable character, as soon as they actually ceased; while the pleasurable emotions produced upon the mind were repeated as often and as long as memory dwelt upon them'.

Dining at The Villa as guests of William Heaven he and his friends learned more about the wild life of the island, including the fact that 'an entomological gentleman, well known to us by reputation' had recently found more than three hundred species of insect, most of them beetles.

On another day, Gosse spent some time alone on the western side of the island, sketching the entrance to a cave; the view, on a bright morning, evoked from him a paragraph of purple prose, which he followed by quoting a poem by that popular poet of Victorian England, Felicia Hemans.

With his companions he visited the deep fissures known as the Earthquake, and walked back by way of Punchbowl Valley. He described a 'basin of the common granite, four feet in diameter, and one in depth, with a uniform thickness of six inches', and discussed its possible use, deciding that it might have been 'the Baptismal font of some very ancient chapel, of which no vestige now remains'. (Today's archeologists suggest that it may represent an abandoned example of the work of millstone cutters who at an as yet unknown time worked on Lundy.)[8]

Gosse's final article provides a description of the lighthouse, just thirty four years after Trinity House had been granted a 999 years lease on its site on Beacon Hill. He had watched 'evening after evening, from the thronged promenade of Capstone Hill, its brilliant torch-like flame' appear and disappear and, watch in hand, counted the intervals. Now he could climb the stone steps to the lantern, a room fifteen feet square, and gaze at the multiple lenses that magnified the brightness of the Argand burner, with its four concentric wicks, and the mechanism that produced the regular occlusion of the light.

Like all lighthouses, Lundy Light attracted all too many birds to their deaths; the keepers told him that sometimes as many as four dozen birds might be found in a single morning, either dead or helpless, outside the lantern.

The lighthouse provided virtually an aerial view of the whole island. It was a day of sun, and the visitors, looking north and east, could see mile upon mile of the coasts on both sides of the Bristol Channel. Nearer at hand a skiff was approaching; it brought news from Ilfracombe that a relation of one of the party was seriously ill. '
'... the case was pressing, the wind was fair, the boat was waiting at the beach; we took a hasty leave of our kind and courteous friend, and were in a few minutes skimming the waves, and looking back to the fast-receding rock, where we had spent a few days of almost unmingled gratification'.

THE MOUSETRAP.

Chapter Nine

Not long before Philip Gosse's visit to Lundy, a workman noticed that the earth sounded hollow at a place at the south end of the island. 'On digging, a block of granite was found a little below the surface; it was about eighteen inches thick, and was estimated to weigh five tons. Its ends rested on two upright slabs, enclosing a cavity some six feet deep and as many wide. It was evident that the excavation had been made and the stones placed by human labour, and the latter operation must have been one of no small difficulty from the great weight of the slabs; but for what purpose it could have been made, there was no clue to inform us,' Gosse noted, adding that all that had been found in the hole was a fragment of pottery, and although the earth at one end was black 'and of an unctuous appearance', there had been no trace of bones.

Chanter, quoting Gosse's account, correctly calls the structure a kistvaen or sepulchral chamber. He goes on to describe a more remarkable find. Either by a slip of the pen, or an unnoticed misprint, he attributes it to 1850 (in which case Gosse would undoubtedly have written about it). In fact, it happened in 1856, according to a record left by William Heaven.[2] Workmen digging foundations for a wall near some of the farm buildings found several skeletons about two feet below the surface. Just one of them was enclosed within a rough tomb of granite and slate slabs, and measured eight feet seven inches 'from the top of the skull to the feet'. Unfortunately the numerous bones found were broken and jumbled together, and on touch and exposure nearly all of them fell to pieces (the fragments were reburied). Heaven says he was not present when the discovery was first made, although he evidently arrived not long afterwards, and tried unsuccessfully to fit together the giant's thigh bones.

His somewhat incoherent account conflicts in several respects with Chanter's, which is surprising since the latter was presumably relying on information given him by Hudson Heaven at the time he was writing his HISTORY OF LUNDY. Chanter speaks of two stone coffins, not one, placed side by side, one ten feet long containing a perfect skeleton measuring eight feet two inches, the other eight feet long containing a skeleton 'several inches above average height . . . imagined to be that of a woman'. When the taller skeleton had been measured, one of the workmen, a man of average height, took up a shin bone and held it against his own leg: 'it reached more then halfway up his thigh from his foot, and the lower jaw easily fitted over his lower jaw outside his beard, whiskers and all'. Chanter speaks of seven other skeletons lying in a line with the stone graves 'but without coffins and of the ordinary stature, and then came a mass of bones of all sorts and sizes, as if many corpses of men, women and children had been thrown indiscriminately into a common grave or pit, with a large quantity of limpet shells lying over them'. Some glass beads found among the bones are now in Bristol Museum, and have been dated to the 9th century A.D., but most of the burials are thought by 20th century archeologists to belong to the periods between the 14th and 17th centuries. One might wish that the mysterious giant, or giants, had not been discovered until a hundred years or so later, when professional archeologists could have examined and reported on them. In the years since the Second World War there have been a number of digs on the south end of Lundy, as well as in other parts of the island; these have established the existence of two early Christian cemeteries on Beacon Hill, but nothing as dramatic as the so-called Giants' Graves has come to light.

Although the Heaven family seems to have lived comfortably enough, with several servants to wait on them at The Villa, a carriage in which to drive around the island, and money to spare for holidays on the mainland and abroad, William Heaven appears to have been anxious to think of ways to make Lundy a paying proposition. Possibly the attempt to establish oyster beds, mentioned by Gosse, was one of them. Reflecting that the island was virtually a solid block of granite, apart from the small area of slate at the south end, its self-styled Squire saw a useful possibility: the island could be made to earn a living out of its own substance.

Samples of Lundy granite were sent to London, and aroused interest; as a result the Lundy Granite Company was registered in 1863, with a reported capital of £100,000. Workmen were recruited — many of them from Scotland — and temporary wooden buildings were put up to house them, although some men were accommodated in the three cottages Heaven had built within the walls of the castle.

Gradually the company carried out a good deal of building: cottages, a store near the farmhouse with a dwelling for the storekeeper, a bakery with living space for the baker, offices for the overseer and timekeeper, a hospital, with a resident surgeon (having regard, no doubt, the fact that quarry workers were liable to frequent injuries). A small jetty was constructed, with a horse-drawn tramway sloping steeply down to carry truckloads of stone. All this work was on the eastern side of the island, where several trial quarries were opened. Much of the company's capital was wasted on these, as the granite taken from them was said not to be of the required quality.

However, large quantities of stone were extracted in the next two or three years and shipped to the mainland aboard the company's own steamer, the *Vanderbyl*, which usually discharged at Fremington quay. On return journeys, she acted as supply ship.[3]

An erroneous tradition arose that Lundy granite was used in the construction of the Thames embankment; directories and guide books published in the late 19th and early 20th centuries repeat this. In fact, it seems that much of the stone was sold for use in Devon. Having leased the greater part of the island, excluding an area on the south-east surrounding The Villa and the castle, together with enough land to provide some kind of smallholding on which his family's needs in the way of farm and vegetable produce could be grown, William Heaven received rent as well as royalties on the tonnage of granite sold.

Within five years the Lundy Granite Company's venture proved uneconomic, and it went into liquidation. Legal complications followed and dragged on for three years, during which time Heaven could not even recover the use of the land that had been included in the lease. As Chanter put it, the company took on themselves 'the occupation and working of the farms, but sadly neglected them, deteriorating the land, and greatly reducing the stock, and in fact causing considerable damage generally by the rough and mischievous conduct of their quarrymen and labourers, so that on the closing of the works everything had retrograded, and it has taken several years to restore things to their former positions'.

In view of his previous jealous concern for the privacy and integrity of the island, it seems surprising that Heaven invited so radical an invasion, however much he may have persuaded himself that he needed the money it might bring. In the event, it seems that it did not benefit him greatly.

Yet surely no one who cares for Lundy can regret its collapse. What would the eastern side of the island — or indeed the island as a whole — have been like today if quarrying had continued for many years? As it is, the abandoned workings appear as comparatively small scars, and have the special quality of romantic melancholy possessed by places recovering after industrial wounding.

Less than thirty years after the Granite Company had left, a visitor wrote: 'Everywhere the hillside is scarred with the excavations; here and there piles of rock lie just as they were when working ceased. The slopes below the road are disfigured with great heaps of refuse, stretching in some places right down to the sea, and it will be years, perhaps centuries, before vegetation can make any appreciable impression upon these sterile heaps.' The jetty had long been washed away, and 'even the solid wall at its base is little more than a ruin'.[4]

The disruption of their former quiet and sedate life by the noises and traffic of the quarries can hardly have been welcome to any of the people living at The Villa; they must also have been grieved at the sight of the desolation on the farms. However, a new source of disturbance was to become familiar in the last decades of the 19th century: the excursion steamer.

Steam power was adapted to drive ships very early in the 19th century. In fact a patent 'Steam Engines, propelling Vessels' was granted in 1779, and by 1812 the first commercially viable steam packet, the *Comet*, was plying in British waters. In the following year the *Charlotte*, with a four-horse-power engine, was built in Bristol, and began to make daily trips on the Avon. By 1823 steam packets were running from Bristol to Ireland, and from then on development was rapid.

Operators soon realized that they could use their little steamships as pleasure craft. In 1827 one of these, the *Lady Rodney*, arrived in Barnstaple on a day in July, 'the first steam vessel that ever came over the bar. Sailed on the following morning for Lundy Island, with a party'.[5] (The *Lady Rodney*, built in 1823, operated from Newport, and usually ran between Newport and Bristol, though she made trips not only to Barnstaple and Lundy, but to Flat Holm, Barry Island and Minehead.)

Bigger steamers capable of carrying more and more passengers were built. In 1867 a Bristol ship owner, James Pockett, bought a two-funnelled iron paddle steamer called the *Velindra*, and until the 1890's used her in summer to make trips to north Devon and Lundy.[6]

At times the behaviour of passengers landing from pleasure steamers made them unpopular, especially if they had been drinking during the crossing from Ilfracombe. Some caused damage on the farm, or harassed the seabirds in the breeding season. William Heaven made an effort to prohibit 'excursionists' from landing at all. When one of the Bristol Steam Navigation's ships, the *Princess Royal*, anchored off the landing beach on July 28th, 1870, he sent a boat to hand a written protest to the captain.

'I hereby give you notice not to land any passengers on my property — the island — or I shall consider you a wilful trespasser and hold you responsible for such purpose, and I hereby inform you that there is no public pathway or road on the Property'. He signed himself 'W. H. Heaven, sole proprietor of this island'.

The captain asked the passengers their wishes, 'and there was a unanimous request for a boat to take them ashore — each one taking

Plate 6

Millcombe House

upon himself the responsibility. Mr. Heaven was on the beach, and made a vigorous protest against persons going up the Trinity House roadway (constructed in 1819) to the lighthouse. Several very curtly told him "the public had the right of way on the island before his time and would have it after him", Mr. Heaven remarking that "he supposed he must submit to mob law".'One passenger subsequently wrote to the 'Bideford Gazette' complaining that some people had behaved disgustingly on the way home;the immense quantities of drink consumed during the day 'made it exceedingly unpleasant and annoying to those who know how to conduct themselves'.[7]

For William Heaven it was an impossible situation. He might call himself the squire, but there was no way in which he could, like some mainland squires, ensure that his estate remained inviolate. Yet the day of the pleasure steamer was to be a long one, and before long day visitors would be warmly welcomed for the money they brought to the island.

In 1875, staying on the mainland with his constant companion, his daughter Amelia (Millie), William Heaven suffered a stroke. He lived for another eight years, but without the power of speech and able to walk only with support. From the time he was well enough to return to Lundy, in July, 1876, he had a nurse and doctor in attendance. A cousin, Mrs. Langworthy (ne Sarah Heaven) met the medical expenses.

From then on it was necessary for his eldest son, the Rev. Hudson Heaven, to take over the running of the island, but he had no sort of training for the task, and was too unworldly and unbusinesslike to make a success of it. His method of dealing with bills he could not pay was to hide them away. Sometimes Mrs. Langworthy had to come to his rescue, although in her opinion the sensible course would have been to sell the island.

The farm, at least, had been restored to order and even improved by an efficient manager appointed by William Heaven in the 1870s, once he had regained control of the area leased to the granite company. Unfortunately this manager was elderly, and after 1879 was forced to give up. The census of 1881 shows that the farmhouse was occupied by Henry Tidball, a shepherd; his wife is described as servant and dairymaid, and the eldest of their seven children as stableboy. A blacksmith with his wife and three children lived at No. 1, Farm Cottages, and a farm labourer named Robert Blackmore was living in the Big House, the south wing of the farmhouse which had been added by the quarry company. His son was also an agricultural labourer, his daughter was a milkmaid, and they had three lodgers who are all described as general labourers. The occupants of The Villa were William Heaven, Hudson Heaven (described as 'priest, without cure'), Amelia, now 47, and the nineteen-year-old Marion, or Winnie, Heaven, whose mother, also Marion, had died two years earlier at the age of 39. (Cecilia Heaven had died in the same year.) They had a cook, housemaid and laundrymaid to look after them, as well as a nurse for William Heaven. The total number of people living on the island, including the three lighthouse keepers and their wives and children (two of them babies only a few weeks old) was sixty. There were nineteen unoccupied dwellings, thirteen of them being the Quarter Wall cottages that had once housed quarry workers.

William Heaven died in 1883. Two years later, with the help of the ever-generous Mrs. Langworthy and other relations, Hudson Heaven began to realize a long-held ambition to build a church on Lundy. At first he could only afford a small corrugated iron structure in Millcombe Valley. As it was classified as a temporary building, it could not be consecrated, but the Bishop of Exeter crossed to he island to dedicate it. He made a jocular reference to it as a 'corrugated irony'; one may wonder whether Hudson Heaven appreciated the quip.

The islanders called it the tin tabernacle. Although to his face they accorded the island's owner the title of Squire, like his father, behind his back they called him Old Daddy Heaven, looking askance as the partiality he showed — however decorous his behaviour — for a boy on the island.

From the time the tin tabernacle was dedicated, Hudson Heaven adopted the courtesy title of vicar, rather than curate-in-charge, as previously. In 1895 he received a legacy of £5,000 — a very large sum at the time, and one that would have relieved him of all money worries for the foreseeable future. Instead, he used it to build another church, of stone: the church of St. Helena that stands on Lundy today.

Building began in September, 1895, and by October of the following year the 'Ilfracombe Chronicle' was reporting that it was 'truly a handsome, if small, fabric . . . built of granite quarried on the island, with stone dressings to windows and doors. Over the Nave entrance there is a splendidly carved statue of St. Helen, the patron saint of Mr. Heaven's kingdom . . . The building is lined with brick of three colours — red, as a body, with buff and blue to relieve it. The Chancel rises two steps, and the Altar two steps. The Choir stalls are of English oak, as well as the reading desk. On the left. looking East, is a finely-chiselled stone pulpit, while the font, with local granite base, is a beautiful bit of workmanship. The architect is Mr. John Norton . . . and the contractors are Messrs. Britton and Pickett, of Ilfracombe . . . The reredos and statue of St. Helen, is by a well-known firm of sculptors, Messrs. H. Hems and Son, of Exeter. The roof of the structure is covered with tiles from Tetbury in Gloucestershire, harmonizing splendidly with the granite walls.'

The church was consecrated on the 7th June, 1897, by the Bishop of Exeter, Dr. Bickersteth. He and fellow clergy, with the choir of St. Sidwells, Exeter, arrived on the paddle steamer *Brighton*. They had a rough crossing, and the bishop is credited with a wry joke: he had almost been persuaded of the existence of purgatory, he said, by experiencing the trials involved in reaching the kingdom of Heaven. A photograph was taken of the choir, with Hudson Heaven standing proudly in their midst, his face encircled by white whiskers, beard and hair.

The church can seat a congregation of 165. There can have been few occasions since its completion when every pew was filled (one of them was the Thanksgiving Service on 25th September, 1969, to mark the acquisition of Lundy by the National Trust) but Hudson Heaven may well have looked to a time when the island's population increased again, as in the years of the Lundy Granite Company's presence.

By this time nothing of the old church of St. Helen remained above ground. Chanter had recorded that 'The walls, which were well built, and with the same peculiar clay cement as the Castle and round towers, are now nearly levelled to the ground, the final destruction having been wrought by the persons conducting the Ordnance Survey, who occupied the site as their signal station, using the stones of the old wall for their cairn'. Hudson Heaven told a reporter from a local paper that his father had been away at the time, but had been very angry when he heard what had happened.

Other important building had been going on since 1895. It had been apparent for some time that the choice of Beacon Hill as the site of a lighthouse, however logical as the highest point of the island, had been a mistake; as Gosse had noted, the peculiarity of the island's climate caused the light to be obscured in fog when the cliffs far below were clear. Trinity House therefore decided to build a lighthouse at each end of the island. The timber barracks put up for the quarry workers had gone; two new ones were built, 'each having berths in tiers of three for twenty-four men,' the Bideford Gazette reported in June, 1895. 'There is a good living room in the centre, with kitchen, and a cook is attached to each house. A proportion of the men are Cornish. The Superintendent of Works is Mr. William Williams, who had lately superintended the building of a lighthouse at Gibraltar'.

Work at the South Light went ahead fairly quickly, as the rock was shale and easy to cut; at the north end the need to cut into granite slowed progress. This probably accounts for the fact that while the North Light is said to have cost £45,000 to complete, the South Light was only £40,000. The new lights were seen for the first time on 18th November, 1897. In Ilfracombe, and probably elsewhere on the coast, people watched expectantly as daylight faded. Suddenly the lights flashed out into the early November darkness, and it may be imagined that many of the watchers cheered: at last Lundy could give shipping a good warning of its presence by night.

Chapter Ten

During the twenty-five years after the death of William Heaven the farm on Lundy was leased by three tenants in succession. The first was T. H. Wright, who lived in the Big House and became the island's first sub-postmaster, using the store as a post office. After six years he left, to be followed in 1891 by a Bideford man named Ackland. The writer of an article called 'Lonely Lundy' which appeared in the 'North Devon Journal' in August, 1898, remarked that 'the hospitable store of Mr. Ackland soon sets us at peace with humanity. Strange to say, you lack for nothing here. There is a fine dining hall, for as many as one hundred steamer visitors sit down to lunch at one time. Everything is provided on the island, and a free kingdom is Lundy. Here the excise troubleth not, and the taxpayer is at rest. Mr. Ackland brews his own beer, without let or hindrance, kills his own bullock or sheep, and bakes his own bread'.

However, Mr. Ackland left in his turn, and was followed by another Bideford man, George John Taylor, of Abbotsham Court, who did not live on the island, but visited it once or twice a month. Writing in the 'Pall Mall Gazette' in 1905, he said that he had leased Lundy from Mr. Heaven for 25 years. During the past seven years, he said, 'I have had a steamer running from Swansea and Ilfracombe to Lundy three times a week from June to September. She has taken 2,500 passengers to Lundy yearly . . . You can get anything you may require on Lundy. I have a large luncheon room capable of seating 250 persons, and each excursion day luncheon is provided. Menu: lobster, lamb, beef, rabbit pie for two shillings. A mail boat goes every week, all the year round, from Instow, taking stores, bread, beef, beer, etc. plus mail. There are only 25 inhabitants on the island: ten belong to me, five to the Government (lighthouses), four Post Office; the rest are Mr. Heaven's people. I have a large boarding house (17 bedrooms). I have 150 bullocks, 500 sheep, some colts, goats etc.' Sportsmen were invited to come to the island to shoot pheasant, woodcock and snipe.

George Taylor (whose use of the possessive may be some indication of his character, and who was not the owner of the *Brighton*, as he implied)[1] converted the Big House into the Manor House Hotel. He was the first to introduce a charge for ferrying passengers ashore from the pleasure steamers. It is possible that his main reason for leasing the island was the hope that he might re-open the granite quarries, but his attempt to float a company failed and, perhaps finding Lundy less profitable than he had expected, he gave up his lease in 1908, when it had run for only ten of the projected twenty five years.

A dramatic event in 1906 may have increased the takings in his luncheon room and boarding house, however. In the issue of the 'North Devon Journal' for 31st May, 1906, a column on the back page (the front page in those days was given over to advertisements) announced in large type 'Battleship Ashore on Lundy'. Subheadings ran 'H.M.S. *Montagu* much damaged. Little hope of refloating. Crew safe'.

The 14,000-ton twin-screw battleship *Montagu* had been launched at Devonport in 1901 and completed in 1903. In May, 1906, she was taking part in manoeuvres in the Bristol Channel. She had been assigned to make trials of what was then called 'wireless telegraphic signalling apparatus'. When thick fog came down as she approached the coast of north Devon her commanding officer, Captain Adair, anchored some miles from Lundy. Later, deciding that there was a danger of a merchant vessel colliding with the ship in very poor visibility, he ordered that she sail nearer the island. Even the bright beam of the South Light did not pierce the fog — nor, surprisingly, were its fog detonators heard. The navigating officer was of the opinion that the *Montagu* was four miles from Hartland when at 2.10 a.m., she struck the Shutter Reef and was held fast.[2]

A landing party managed to climb the cliffs — a hazardous undertaking at any time, but exceptionally so at night, in fog. Reaching the top they turned north, drawn by the sound of the North

Light's sirens. When they finally reached the lighthouse at about 5.30 a.m., the officer in charge was so positive that they were on the mainland that he had a heated argument with the keeper, who finally clinched matters by saying, 'Do you suppose I don't know which bloody lighthouse I'm keeping?'

As soon as the news of the *Montagu's* stranding had been wired to the mainland by Lloyd's agent on the island, the Admiralty ordered her sister ship H.M.S. *Duncan* (which had been coaling with her at Cardiff before the manoeuvres) to steam to her assistance. Other naval vessels were diverted to Lundy. By the 7th June a correspondent of the 'Western Morning News', who had managed to reach Lundy by the mail boat (Captain Dark's *Gannet*) was reporting a remarkable assembly of naval ships: another battleship, the *Exmouth*, the cruiser *Dido* and destroyers *Kennet* and *Ribble*. There were also salvage tugs. Divers were at work; they found that the *Montagu* had been pierced by rocks in several places; the engine-room, stokehole and other compartments were flooded, and both propellers had been smashed. Although for a time plans were put forward to repair and refloat the ship, it eventually became apparent that she would have to be abandoned. She had been carrying £10,000 in specie, and this had been taken off her on the day she went aground and stored for twenty-four hours at The Villa before being transferred to *Duncan*.

Not one of the ship's crew of between 700 and 800 men had been lost, and all were quickly transported to the mainland. Salvage work continued for months. Once the ship's guns and other vital equipment had been taken ashore by naval salvors, she was auctioned. A South Wales company bought her for £4,250 and, housing their workers in the Marisco Castle cottages, proceeded to dispose of large quantities of armour plate, copper and brass at a considerable profit until little remained but the great steel hull.

In the following August Captain Adair and his navigating officer, Lieut. Dathan, were court-martialled. The charge was that they 'by negligence or default, did hazard, strand or lose their ship'. Both were found guilty, severely reprimanded and dismissed their ship —

a somewhat redundant punishment in the circumstances. Lieut. Dathan also lost two years seniority.

Throughout the summer of 1906 the paddle steamer companies ran dozens of trips carrying sightseers who were, it seems, less interested in visiting Lundy than in gazing at what remained of the Navy's most expensive peacetime loss in westcountry waters. Gradually the sea worked at the huge hulk. Within a few years only a little of it appeared above water; by 1922 only her barbettes were visible at very low tide. Today, it is necessary to be a diver to see what is left of her.

By the beginning of the 20th century the once large family group at The Villa had dwindled to three — Hudson Heaven and his only surviving sister, Millie, and one of their father's cousins, Annie. None of the younger members of the family remained: William Heaven's Australian-born granddaughter, Winnie, baptised Marion after her mother, had married in 1888 without changing her surname: her husband was a cousin, John Cookesley Heaven. From then on she had lived in Bristol. Her brother Walter had also left the island. After Millie's death in 1905, a niece of Cousin Annie came to care for the ageing pair, and Walter, who had emigrated to Australia, came back with his young second wife to take over the management of the island.

In 1911 Hudson Heaven, with Cousin Annie, moved to Torrington. He died in 1916, in his 90th year. On a cold February day his body was brought back to the island aboard the cutter *Gannet*, on which he had often enjoyed sailing with Captain Dark.

His coffin, surrounded by candles and flowers, was left overnight in the church he had built, and the next day was carried to his grave by islanders.[3] The only family members present were Winnie and her husband and Walter and his wife; the latter couple had been living, not at The Villa, but at the farmhouse. (Kellys Directory for 1914 has the simple entry 'Walter Charles Hudson Heaven, farmer, farmhouse')

After the funeral, Winnie recorded in her diary, 'We soon started for the beach, lingering to look in the windows of the empty house

Plate 7

Victorian paddle steamers

(The Villa) as we passed down the road — Walter never goes that way to the beach otherwise. I think, like myself, it is too full of poignant memories, and saddened with the knowledge the voices we loved and heard there are for ever still . . . and yet their presences unseen, unheard are felt in every room'.

Walter inherited Lundy but, like his uncle, lacked the sort of abilities or training that might have enabled him to succeed in the difficult task of living on the island. Within a year he was bankrupt, and so, eighty years after it had been bought by William Heaven, Lundy was put up for sale.

With the First World War in progress, it was not easy to find a buyer, but in 1918 Augustus Langham Christie of Tapeley Court, Instow, became its owner.

Christie was descended from the Cleveland family. When John Cleveland (or Clevland, as he spelled his name) the long-serving M.P. for Barnstaple who had owned Lundy in the 18th century, died childless in 1817, at the age of 83, his heir was his nephew, Augustus Saltren Willett Christie, an army officer. A window in Instow church commemorates Augustus Clevland, of Tapely Park, Deputy Lieutenant of Devon, a hero of Waterloo who died in 1849, and his son Cornet Archibald Clevland of the 17th Lancers, 'one of the renowned 500 in the Battle of Balaclava', as the inscription records. Having survived the Charge of the Light Brigade (one of only three officers to do so) he died of wounds received a few days later at the battle of Inkerman. He was 21 years old. (His portrait may be seen at Tapeley Park today, with his sword, service cap, a replica of his helmet and a ring he sent to his mother.) It was his sister Agnes who took Tapeley into the possession of the Christie family by marrying William Augustus Christie of Glydebourne in Sussex.[4]

Augustus Christie did not live on Lundy. It was leased by Herbert May, of Shirwell Park in north Devon, a successful stock breeder. May also leased the *Lerina*, the vessel with which Christie had replaced the stalwart *Gannet*, which had carried stores and the mails to Lundy, and passengers to and from the mainland, for some 45 years. A writer in the 1890s spoke of the *Gannet* as 'a fine seaworthy craft, commanded, too, by as handsome a son of Devon as you will find between Glenthorne and Marsland — a skipper tall and straight and sunburnt, with brown beard and clear blue eye', and sixteen years later a journalist described the same skipper as 'A fine type of Devonian, well set up, well preserved, the picture of robust health, with expressive blue eyes beaming with kindliness, whilst grey hair and pointed beard impart distinction to a strong countenance'.[5]

This excellent seaman was William Dark, born in 1848 at Woolfardisworthy (Woolsery), near Bideford. As a young man he had served in the Lundy Granite Company's *Vanderbyl*. In 1874, having bought the *Gannet* off the stocks, he entered into an agreement with William Heaven to carry stores and mail from Instow to Lundy. His son Fred, one of his ten children, had sailed as mate on the *Gannet* for many years, and in 1919 was appointed captain of the *Lerina*; William Dark, now over 70, was ready to retire.

The *Lerina* was a former Lowestoft drifter. Augustus Christie had her stripped, overhauled and refitted; there was accommodation for passengers which included a ladies' cabin. However, although the 'North Devon Journal' reported in August, 1922, that she was 'certified by the Board of Trade to carry some 80-odd passengers over the Bar', the number was in fact restricted to twelve, as Fred Dark held only a 'fishing ticket'.

It is possible that one of the passengers carried on the *Lerina* at some time in the early 1920s was the then popular novelist and playwright Clemence Dane (Winifred Ashton) who took her pen name from the London church of St. Clement Dane. In 1926 she had some success with a play called GRANITE. The scene, throughout, is 'the living room of Jordan Morris's farm on Lundy . . . a large vaulted room that has been the kitchen of a 12th century castle'. The time is just after the end of the Napoleonic wars, and the principal characters are Jordan himself, a churlish middle-aged man, his wife Judith, considerably younger and resentful of her husband, and the latter's handsome young half-brother Prosper, recently discharged from the navy. There is also a sixteen-year-old servant, Penny Holt.

It is a melodramatic piece in which Judith, on a night of violent storm, offers to sell her soul to the devil for the sake of Prosper's love, and the devil duly appears in the guise of a shipwrecked man. He is referred to throughout the play simply as the Man. He shoots Jordan, making it look like an accident. Prosper sells the farm he owns on the mainland and returns to marry Judith. To her dismay, he chooses to stay on Lundy to farm and open granite quarries. She soon becomes jealous, suspecting him of becoming attracted to Penny, and they quarrel. The Man pushes Prosper over the cliffs, and the terrified Judith is left in his power.

It would seem that Clemence Dane based this play on a story called 'Cruel Coppinger', by Robert Stephen Hawker, vicar of Morwenstow. He included it in his FOOTPRINTS OF FORMER MEN IN FAR CORNWALL. It tells of a Dutchman who comes ashore from a ship wrecked at Hartland (the sole survivor), marries a local girl and ill-treats her. This in turn had a historical basis: a naval seaman called Daniel Herbert Coppinger was shipwrecked on 23rd December, 1792, was taken in by a local family, made a living for a time as a smuggler, and was declared bankrupt in 1802.[6]

Like earlier owners of Lundy, Augustus Christie was aware that it would be a convenience to have a well-constructed pier or jetty. He decided to have one built. A dozen men, mostly from Devon and Cornwall, arrived in June, 1920, and set to work in the Cove. During the eleven months they were on the island they helped to form a football team, called the Pirates of Lundy, and even a Lundy Band which played on special occasions such as a farewell party for someone leaving the island, or what the 'Hartland Chronicle ' described as 'an open air entertainment on Lundy Green' in July, 1921, at which the band 'gave selections, which were very much appreciated.'

Although the permanent population of Lundy remained small (numbering 48 in 1921) the islanders seem to have acquired a new sense of community. Under the ownership of William Heaven and his eldest son, the island had been in effect a tiny agricultural village observing the forms of the Victorian squirearchy. There had been a clear divide between the family at The Villa and the other islanders — including the lighthouse keepers, whose presence was probably resented, since it represented an intrusion by mainland authority. Now social life, helped undoubtedly by the arrival of the pier builders, became livelier. Another influence was the manageress of the Manor House Hotel, Miss Nancy Sage. Evidently an excellent caterer who enjoyed her work, she was happy to organise events such as whist drives, concerts, parties and dances.

She also helped to look after the church of St. Helena, decorating it with flowers for festivals. From the time the Rev. Heaven left Lundy, there was no incumbent. From 1913 to 1916 the Rev. William Swatridge had been curate-in-charge, living on the island, but his fondness for the bottle and his habit of terrorising his wife had made him an unwelcome cleric. However, the church was devoutly cared for by a naval pensioner, Frederick William Allday. He had been born in Lewisham in 1858, but after his naval service had moved to Instow. He applied to Lloyds, was accepted for training and appointed to the Signal Station on Lundy in October, 1896. He also became the island's postman. (A minute from Sir S. A. Blackwood, Secretary to the Post Office, dated 15th April, 1896, refers to an application by Trinity House and the Committee of Lloyds in support of an application from the lessee of Lundy, who would have been Mr. Ackland, for the establishment of a postal service. He recommended approval 'to develop the resources and promote the convenience of the Island', provided that suitable provisions could be made for an office).[7] (The first known hand franking stamp for Lundy bears the date 1896) When Allday made a brief visit to Ilfracombe in 1920 to consult a doctor, it was the first time he had left the island since his arrival there 24 years earlier, and it would seem that he could not wait to return.[8] He had been a custodian of the church since 1911, when the Rev. Heaven withdrew to the mainland; in 1918 he had become licensed lay reader. He conducted services and preached sermons, but according to the 'Ilfracombe Chronicle' of December 10th, 1921, the islanders were 'at present hoping for the speedy discovery of a clergyman all their own'. In the same month the 'Hartland Chronicle' reported that 'The Bishop of Crediton, who has spent some weeks on the island, is seeking for a clergyman who will make Lundy his home. Though full of romance, it is a lonely spot, and the stipend would be small, but the position might appeal to a bachelor of studious habits, and who is fond of the sea'.

In June, 1922, the Rev. Henry Hezekiah Lane, formerly curate of Neils Harbour, Cape Breton, and more recently priest in charge of Welcome, near Hartland, was licensed as domestic chaplain to the Bishop of Exeter and put in charge of Lundy and all visiting ships. He was inducted as rector of Lundy by Dr. Trefusis, Bishop of Crediton, in the following August. A congregation of about sixty attended, including several north Devon clergy, the choirs of Ilfracombe parish church and St. James's church, a band of ringers and a number of visitors who crossed on the *Devonia*.

In an interview, Mr. Lane was reported as saying that the bells had never been rung, as there was no band of ringers on the island; he was initiating some of the islanders into the mysteries of campanology.[9] He was mistaken, however: as an inscription in the church records, a peal of Steadman Triples was rung by the Gloucester and Bristol Association of Change Ringers soon after the church was consecrated, and more recently members of the Lundy football team and visiting ringers from mainland parishes had rung the bells. In July, 1921, a Mr. Reed from Shirwell had 'found the bells in excellent order, and had taught a set of young ringers to chime the bells'.[10]

When Mr. Lane presided over his first vestry meeting in January, 1923, Miss Sage was appointed Rector's Warden and William Allday became parish clerk and sexton. However, there were not to be many such meetings under Mr. Lane's rectorship. Although he was quoted as saying, on the day of his induction, that he was not afraid that he would find the life on Lundy lonely, as he was a lover of nature and isolation, and there was much work he intended to do, by June, 1924, he had resigned. It may be that he found his stipend too meagre: it consisted of £60 provided by the Ecclesiastical Commissioners with a similar amount raised by the church at large.

More changes were to begin in the following year. In October, 1925, Augustus Christie sold Lundy to Martin Coles Harman, and the islanders soon became aware that the new owner was quite as autocratic as William Heaven had been, if not more so.

ENTRANCE TO THE CAVERN.

Chapter Eleven

Martin Coles Harman was born in Surrey in 1895, one of the eleven children of a builder from Arundel.[1] Perhaps significantly, he took his middle name from his mother, Florence Coles; she was Devonian, born in Honiton, and had been a schoolteacher before her marriage. At the age of eighteen Martin visited Lundy on one of the pleasure steamers of the White Funnel Fleet, and afterwards assured a friend that one day he would buy the island. Two years earlier he had begun his working life as an office boy with the bankers, Lazard Brothers. Energy, ability and ambition — helped, perhaps, by the fact that he did not serve in the First World War — resulted in his becoming, by the time he was 33, a director of Lazards and a member of the Institute of Bankers. In the early 1920s he went into business on his own with such success that he quickly became a rich man. In 1925, seeing Lundy advertised for sale by auction, he made an offer of £16,000 to buy it by private treaty. Thus by the age of 40 he had fulfilled his youthful resolve.

In the following year Felix Gade, a friend he had known since boyhood, and who was also related to him by marriage (his elder brother had married Gade's sister) became his resident agent. In his long and detailed autobiography, MY LIFE ON LUNDY, Felix Gade reveals great loyalty to, and admiration of, his employer — and yet makes it apparent that Harman, like many men of unusual financial acumen, was strong-willed and forceful. However, he was 'easily approachable and never put on side. He always remained a countryman, but by force of intellect and character he could hold his own with any assembly'. Moreover, he had 'an inexhaustible supply of impish vitality . . . He seemed to have retained his youthful capacity for excitement and adventure, and it manifested itself in his jealous guardianship of, and pride in, his small kingdom'.

Harman, like William Heaven, had bought Lundy for his private pleasure and that of his family and friends. He had no wish to attempt any kind of destructive development, but he considered that the island should be as far as possible self-supporting. It was his agent's business to achieve this, yet Harman's impulsive and often impractical ideas tended to get in the way. On the island when he bought it were cattle, goats, sheep, pigs, and poultry. He proceeded to introduce pea-fowl, a hundred pheasants, 200 Irish geese, some red grouse, Angora and Chinchilla rabbits, a few red squirrels, and three varieties of deer. There had been fallow deer on Lundy since the 18th century, if not earlier; now more were added, as well as red and Sika deer. Dogs were another matter: Martin Harman disliked them, and would have preferred to have none on the island, but compromised by stipulating that all must be of the same sex — bitches, as it turned out, He did his best to eliminate the large number of semi-wild cats by offering five shillings for every cat brought in to be killed. In consequence the ever-present nuisance of rats and rabbits increased rapidly, and a few cats were permitted once more. Few of the birds and smaller animals survived; only the deer, after early casualties, were able to multiply.

The pheasants, of course, were brought to the island to be shot in due course. On the Christmas Day following their arrival, Martin Harman and two friends set out with guns. A pheasant fell into tall gorse and, in the absence of a dog, could not be found. To prevent a repetition of this, Harman ordered his agent to fire the undergrowth, although 'it was pointed out to him that, with a brisk east wind, it would be difficult to control a fire of that sort'. The fire burned fiercely for more than 24 hours, spreading a considerable distance along the east side of the island. Workers spent hours creating a firebreak, but only rain finally quenched the smouldering turf.

It was an interesting demonstration of the new owner's impatient, headstrong nature.

His most successful and long-lasting introduction was of ponies.

In keeping with his usual policy of never doing things by halves, he bought 34 New Forest mares, with eight foals, in the autumn of 1928. A small Welsh Mountain stallion sired a few foals, but unfortunately died within a year. One of his sons replaced him as stud, and until their numbers were drastically reduced in the early 1980s, the free-roaming herd gave a special quality to the life of the island.

A short-lived venture that was not Martin Harman's idea was the construction of a nine-hole golf course on Ackland's Moor, the area on the west side of the island to the north of Beacon Hill. It was the suggestion of a visitor who was secretary of a Glamorgan golf club, and was allowed to go ahead because it was thought it might attract custom to the Manor Farm Hotel. The course was opened in July, 1927, but it never drew enough players to make it a paying proposition, and Martin Harman closed it at the end of 1928.

Miss Sage provided a lobster luncheon for the hundred or more golfing enthusiasts who arrived on the day of the opening, but this was one of the last large-scale events for which she catered: she left the island the following October. Felix Gade married Edith Irene Clarke in February, 1928; she had originally come to Lundy as a store keeper, but gradually took over responsibility for the hotel as well as the Marisco Tavern and Store.

Augustus Christie's vessel, the *Lerina*, had been bought at the same time as the island. Fred Dark continued to captain her, and 'never failed to land passengers, mails and freight at some point on the island, no matter from what direction the wind blew'. His expert seamanship and knowledge of the island ensured that he could, if necessary, land at places that many would have thought too hazardous; these included Montagu steps, Smugglers' Path west of Lametry, the Cove, Hell's Gates, Brazen Ward, Frenchman's Landing, Gannet's Bay and the Pyramid. He was called on to transport live animals on a number of occasions, though these had necessarily to be loaded or put ashore at the main landing beach.

In accordance with his intention to put the independence of Lundy beyond doubt, Martin Harman managed to dissuade two government departments, the Post Office and the Admiralty, from continuing their presence on the island by the simple method of demanding double the existing charges. However, he was content to let the mail be carried aboard the *Lerina*, at first at his own expense. In 1929, however, when his business interests had been affected, like so many others, by the stock market crash on Wall Street, it occurred to him that he might issue Lundy stamps. It was of course necessary for letters and packages to any place on the mainland to bear ordinary postage stamps, but Lundy stamps might be used to cover the cost of what was now, in effect, a private post office. Accordingly two designs were prepared and printed by Bradbury Wilkinson, and Co. of New Malden. On November 1st, 1929, the first stamps went on sale, the blue One Puffin and the pink Half Puffin. They were popular with visitors, who seem to have had no objection to paying to adorn their postcards with these attractive stamps, known as puffinage. Before long, as new denominations were added, the Lundy issues began to interest collectors — though some serious philatelists were wary of them initially. Once the Second World War began, it became difficult to supply all those who wanted stamps from the island, and Martin Harman founded the Lundy Philatelic Bureau, in 1941, based first at Northampton and later at Kettering.

It was perhaps the success of the stamps that encouraged him to go a step further, and have one-puffin and half-puffin coins minted. The obverse of both shows a profile head, in relief, of himself, encircled by the inscription 'Martin Coles Harman 1929'. The reverse of the larger coin showed a puffin standing on a rock, with 'Lundy One Puffin' inscribed below; the reverse of the smaller coin simply bore a puffin's head and the words 'Half Puffin'. Neither was milled; instead their edges were inscribed 'Lundy Lights and Leads', a slogan coined by Harman.

Neither the Postmaster General nor, presumably, anyone else had objected to Lundy stamps (although it was stipulated that they should not be affixed on the same side as Royal Mail stamps). But coins were a different matter — especially coins bearing a portrait of someone other than the monarch. Plain clothes policemen visited Lundy to assure themselves that the coins were circulating there, in the Marisco Tavern and Store — there had never been any secret about it — and in April, 1930, Martin Harman was summoned to appear before the Bench of Petty Sessions at Bideford. He duly appeared, but refused to plead, as he denied that the Bench had any right to try a case concerning Lundy. Like William Heaven, he seems to have aspired to a kind of dual identity, as a law-abiding British citizen under the protection of the Crown, and as the unquestioned lord of a private and independent domain.

Initially, his counsel's submission was that Lundy was in fact outside the jurisdiction of any mainland court. The Bench considered this point briefly, decided that it had no validity, and the case proceeded. The reluctant defendant was found guilty, fined five pounds and twenty guineas costs. He responded by saying he would pay under protest, and lodged an appeal. When this was heard in the Kings Bench Division in the autumn of 1930, the decision of the Bideford magistrates was upheld.[2]

Fifty thousand coins of each of the two denominations had been minted by the Birmingham mint, and could not now be used as legal tender. Yet many people showed an interest in them, and no objection was raised to their being sold as curios — at first for a penny or a halfpenny, later at prices which increased until the stock was exhausted.

After the closing of the Signal Station there was some pressure on Martin Harman to accept a coastguard station instead. He resisted this with his usual intransigence, insisting that he could look after his own coasts. He agreed to maintain the rocket life-saving apparatus and arrange for a watch to be kept in bad weather. He also made arrangements to instal a Marconi radio-telephone in the Old Light to connect with the Hartland Point coastguard station; this was linked to the Manor Farm Hotel and the North and South Lights. The island now had a means of communication with the mainland that could be relied on, unlike the cable to the Croyde coastguard, laid in the 1890s, which had broken from time to time.

It happened to be broken in March, 1919, several years before the radio-telephone was installed. On a foggy night a 1,200-ton Greek merchant vessel, the *Maria Kyriakides*, ran on to rocks on the east side of the island, near Tibbett's Point. There was no way of letting anyone on the mainland know what had happened — attempts by the lighthouse keepers to attract the attention of passing ships by firing maroons were unsuccessful — until the *Lerina* arrived a few days later on her usual weekly visit. The *Maria Kyriakides* was eventually repaired and towed away, but the accident was of considerable benefit to the islanders, as the salvage company working on her agreed that they might help themselves to her cargo of coal and a quantity of her stores.

Almost exactly two years later another Greek ship, the *Taxiarchis*, went aground not far from the place where the *Maria Kyriakides* had been stranded. This ship was a total wreck. The crew were rescued using the life-saving apparatus, and again the islanders benefited by being allowed to salvage coal and assorted stores.

Felix Gade's duties had increased: he had become Lloyds' agent on the island, responsible for reporting all arrivals and departures of shipping sheltering in Lundy waters. He was also expected to make twice-daily calls to Hartland coastguards. As there were no vehicles on the island, this would have involved a walk of rather more than a mile, there and back, between the Manor Farm Hotel and the Old Light, twice a day, in addition to his ordinary work.

In his matter-of-fact account of his life during these years, there is little sign that he resented any of the difficulties his position sometimes caused him; his loyalty to his employer was absolute. That loyalty was to receive and unexpected test in 1933. At the beginning of March, national and west country newspapers reported that Martin Coles Harman, aged 47, described as a city financier, had been arrested with three other directors of a company called the Chosen Corporation, and charged with having 'between November 10th, 1930, and August 31st, 1932, unlawfully conspired together with others unknown, to cheat and defraud such persons as were shareholders in Chosen Corporation Ltd.' They were released on bail of £2,000 each.

The Directory of Directors for 1932 shows that Martin Harman was a director, and in some cases chairman, of a dozen companies: Aurochs Investment Co., Branston Artificial Silk Co., British Bank for Foreign Trade, Central Oil, Mining and Chemicals Trust, Colonial Proprietary Co., Gas, Water and General Investment Trust, New African Co., Oceania Consolidated Co., London Irish Trust, Rock Investments Co., and Textile Industrial Trust Co., in addition to the Chosen Corporation.

The trial began at the Central Criminal Court on October 23rd, 1933; the hearing lasted seventeen days, spread over four weeks. According to the 'Daily Telegraph', the prosecution claimed that 'Chosen Corporation shares were sold to Japanese subsidiary companies at excessive prices in order to assist other companies in which Harman was interested'. He was found guilty on all counts and sentenced to eighteen months imprisonment; two of his fellow directors were found not guilty and the third was sentenced to six months. Harman had pleaded not guilty. However his subsequent appeal was dismissed, and he served fourteen months in Wormwood Scrubs. On April 8th, 1935, a few weeks after his release, he was flown to Lundy from the new Barnstaple aerodrome, which had been opened while he was in prison.

Felix Gade's discretion was such that he did not mention this episode in his autobiography. Instead, he represented it as no more than a bankruptcy as a consequence of the slump, and passed over the years 1933 to 1935, merely saying that he continued as Lundy's resident agent, having been asked by the Receiver to manage the island's affairs as usual. Family ownership of the island was secure, as Martin Harman had earlier created a trust for his four children (his wife had died in 1931) which included Lundy.

During his employer's enforced absence, Felix Gade presumably kept him in touch, as far as circumstances allowed, with happenings on Lundy. One question which would have needed a decision concerned the construction of a landing strip. Robert Boyd, who had established the Barnstaple Aerodrome and Flying Club, was eager to begin a regular air service to the island as soon as possible after the aerodrome opened in June, 1934. Gade recorded that ' . . . although

Mr. Harman was not enthusiastic about permitting aeroplanes on Lundy, I managed to persuade him to allow the Ministry of Aviation to license . . . the area between the Lighthouse Wall and the Quarter Wall as a public landing ground'. Although Robert Boyd made several flights to Lundy during the second half of 1934 in one or other of his two Gipsy Moths, and some with passengers in a low-winged monoplane called a Monospar, which could carry four, he did not begin a regular service until he had acquired a twin-engined, six-seater monoplane called a Short Scion. Before this he had wiped off the undercarriage of another aircraft, a De Havilland Dragon, on a wall dividing the landing strip from the area known as Ackland's Moor.

He made a safe belly landing, and no one was hurt, but the Ministry of Aviation decreed that the little airfield should be lengthened. 'Work commenced immediately and was completed within a month by two men, one horse and one two wheeled truck . . . constructed out of sections of salvaged hatch covers, and a pair of old wheels which had been used on the Lundy Granite Company's tramlines' — an interesting example of what could be achieved by simple means before the advent of powered earth-moving machines.

As a subsidy was available for commercial flights carrying passengers and freight, it was possible to keep fares low: initially the return fare from Barnstaple was fifteen shillings (75p), later increased to 17s.6d. (89p) Once the regular service began, Felix Gade recalled, an era of prosperity came to the Manor Farm Hotel. 'Mr. Boyd kept very regular hours and was also often able to make two extra flights in the morning with day trippers'. As he was now carrying the Lundy mails, he decided to bring out some suitable stamps. The first issues were printed in rolls and numbered, so that they have often been referred to as the tram ticket series. Later larger stamps were issued, all values bearing the same design — an aircraft flying towards Lundy, with part of the north Devon coast in the background.

The charge for these stamps meant that Lundy air mail was more expensive than the sea-borne mail, but many people were willing to pay the extra amount for the sake of speed of delivery.

In the Thirties things were going well on Lundy. Under Felix Gade's faithful stewardship the farm was productive; the Campbell pleasure steamers brought hundreds of trippers on every fine summer day, which guaranteed good custom for the Marisco Tavern and the sale of postcards and Lundy stamps, and the Manor Farm Hotel was busy. As for Martin Harman himself, it would seem that once he had regained his freedom it was not long before he obtained his discharge from bankruptcy and somehow managed to return to the life of a successful businessman; certainly there are no indications that he encountered any further financial difficulties. His elder brother Terry, Felix Gade's brother-in-law, had evidently been of great help to him; Gade observed that he had been 'the mainstay of Martin Harman's business after his bankruptcy'.

Yet even on Lundy there was no escape from the shadow that had darkened the whole of Europe during the last years of the Thirties. At the beginning of September, 1939, the Campbell steamer that called at the island was not only the last of the season: it was the last to call there for ten years, and many of those who boarded her must have wondered whether they would ever see Lundy again.

ONE PENNY

Chapter Twelve

With the outbreak of war, all civil flying from Barnstaple Aerodrome came to an end, and Lundy lost the usefully swift air service it had enjoyed for nearly five years. Work began on the air station that was to become RAF Chivenor, on former farmland along the wide levels beside the Taw-Torridge estuary to the east of Braunton. The station opened in October, 1940, as a Coastal Command training base. Before long it was attracting the attention of German aircraft: it was attacked several times during the spring of 1941, and two Heinkels which may have been on their way to bomb Chivenor crashed on Lundy within a few days of one another. The first may have suffered combat damage, although its crew, who all survived, claimed that the cause had been mechanical failure. (The pilot, Elmar Botcher, visited Lundy in June, 1991, and was shown the fragmentary remains of his aircraft.) They were taken to Chivenor for questioning aboard the *Lerina*, guarded by naval ratings. When, on April 1st, someone reported that another Heinkel had crashed, the news was at first taken for to be a joke, but was soon found to be true. This time two of the Germans were dead and a third seriously wounded. The survivors were very glad to be given a protective escort, as the crew of a fishing trawler, the *Kestrel*, who had been recovering on the island after being shot up by a Heinkel (their mate had been killed) were bent on revenge. An armed guard from Chivenor had to be sent for before they could be landed at Appledore; an angry crowd had gathered on the quay, having by some mysterious means learned the identity of the *Lerina's* passengers.

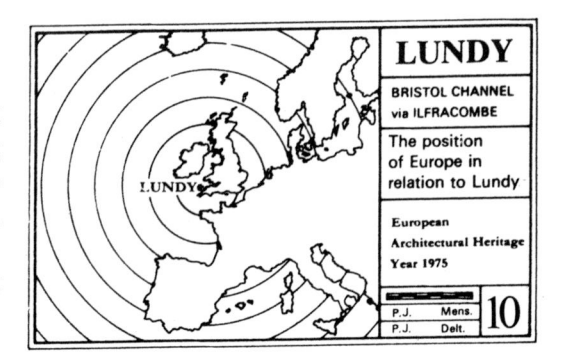

A third crash on Lundy in 1941 was that of a Whitley bomber returning to Chivenor from one of the long, wearying patrols over

Plate 8

Trinity House gunners and their wives at the Battery

the Bay of Biscay that were the regular work of Coastal Command squadrons in the south-west. Sadly, all her crew were killed.

According to Felix Gade, those living on the island saw more evidence of intense activity in the approaches to the Bristol Channel between late March and late June, 1941, than at any other time during the war. In view of its position, it might have been expected that Lundy would be very securely guarded, but a small naval detachment consisting of an elderly lieutenant and six ratings were the only representatives of the armed services on the island. They lived and worked in the Old Light. Its high lantern chamber offered an excellent look-out post; as Gosse discovered almost a century earlier; on a clear day a watcher could gaze out across the whole island, the miles of sea around it and the coasts of the approaches to the Bristol Channel. Anything of importance could be reported immediately to the mainland authorities by the radio-telephone installed in the mid-Thirties.

Lundy was in effect a tiny naval outpost throughout the war. No civilian could cross to the island without the permission of the officer commanding the Appledore area, Rear-Admiral Franklin, and he gave it sparingly. Naval motor launches operating from Appledore had a permanent mooring at Lundy, and their crews often landed on the island when things were quiet. Their arrival towards the end of 1940 put an end to the poaching by French crabbers which continued, astonishingly, after the fall of France in May of that year. This is the more surprising as a large minefield protected the western coasts. (Occasionally mines broke loose and caused alarm by exploding on the rocks of Lundy or the mainland.) The Admiralty commandeered the *Lerina* to serve both as a patrol vessel and as a supply boat for the detachment in the Old Light. Later she was bought from Martin Harman. For some time Fred Dark continued to captain her, but later was appointed naval pilot for the Taw-Torridge estuary. He suffered a heart attack and died in the summer of 1942. The *Lerina's* last war-time service was as a standby vessel serving divers laying the experimental pipe-line across the Bristol Channel, in preparation for the 'Pluto' pipe-lines laid across the English Channel before D-day.

The only criticism of his employer that Felix Gade permitted himself in MY LIFE ON LUNDY was that he was not a good judge of men. This failing was amply demonstrated when he leased the island to a Herbert Van Os in 1940. The latter was said to be disposing of the estate he owned in Middlesex and of commitments in the city of London. Clearly he had a persuasive tongue. He arrived at the end of the year with a party of six, including a Mrs. Leyden, who was to run the hotel, the Marisco Tavern and the Store. Felix Gade and his wife were told to move to Millcombe House, formerly The Villa. The entire management of the island was to be in the hands of Van Os.

It soon became apparent that the new lessee knew virtually nothing of farming (though he claimed to have owned one) and wanted only to make all he could out of the island as quickly as possible. The unhappy agent, prohibited from intervening or advising, had to watch while everything he had worked to build up during the previous decade was run down. Fodder was wasted, animals died, tools and machinery were misused or broken and not repaired or replaced, dozens of deer were shot and their venison sold.

The account given of this episode in MY LIFE ON LUNDY is written with restraint, yet inevitably there is a strong underlying note of bitterness. At last, in February, 1942, Martin Harman — who lived in London during the war — was persuaded to terminate what was to have been a ten-year lease. Van Os and his companions left; Felix Gade took over the farm again, and began the slow work of restoring it, with limited help. Sometimes one or two naval ratings, or the lighthouse keepers, would lend a hand, and a Land Girl arrived who was an excellent worker.

Of the dozen or so people who had been living on the island when the war began, and had watched transports, escorted by destroyers, sailing past on their way to France with men of the British Expeditionary Force, only Felix Gade and his wife were still there when, in June, 1944, a far larger fleet, augmented this time by American ships, passed on its way to begin the invasion of Normandy. The Gades too were to leave before the war ended. Three years of very hard physical works may have aggravated a tendency to sciatica which Felix Gade had suffered for some time, and he accepted his wife's suggestion that it was time seek a slightly less demanding life on the mainland. They took over the management of the Hartland Quay Hotel. Martin Harman, who did not immediately appoint a new agent, 'became almost a regular weekend visitor to the Quay. He liked to discuss Lundy affairs with me' — which suggests that Mr. Gade's knowledge and advice may have continued to have some influence on island life during the four years he spent on the mainland. However, the agent appointed in due course was Donald T. Heysman.

In 1948 a week's holiday on Lundy convinced Mr. Gade and his wife that the island was their real home. On May 2nd, 1949, they were able to return there to manage the hotel. The building had been neglected during and since the war, when both labour and materials were virtually unobtainable. Extensive repairs to roof, walls and ceiling were carried out, and the plumbing was renewed; within a few months the building was ready to receive visitors again.

No Campbell steamers had been landing passengers on Lundy since the end of the war. Trips were run to Lundy Roads, but for several years there were no suitable launches available on the island to ferry people from ship to shore. (Merely to view the island, without landing, sounds a tantalizing outing, but in May, 1948, for instance, nearly 500 day trippers took the opportunity of doing so.)[3]

During the war the steamers, commandeered by the Admiralty, had given good service, acting as minesweepers, bringing men back from the beaches of Dunkirk, and being used as accommodation ships off the Normandy coast after the D-day landings. Five were lost, and when the survivors were released from naval duties, two were in such a bad state that they had to be scrapped. It was possible to refit just three for excursions in 1946; in addition, a new paddler, the *Bristol Queen*, was launched in the autumn of that year, her rapid construction a remarkable feat in those day of shortages. Places along the Bristol Channel, including Ilfracombe, happily welcomed the trade brought by passengers, but Lundy had to wait — until, on June 20th, 1949, the *Glen Gower* arrived. Many of those aboard her had come for a special occasion: the unveiling of a memorial to Martin Harman's elder son on the fifth anniversary of the publication of the citation, in the 'London Gazette', of the posthumous award of the V.C. to Lance Corporal John Pennington Harman of the Queen's Own Royal West Kent Regiment.

At the battle of Kohima John Harman had been commanding a section of a forward platoon. When fire from an enemy machine gun post endangered his Company, John Harman had gone forward alone, destroyed the post with a grenade and brought the machine gun back. The following morning he charged another enemy group and killed several in hand-to-hand fighting, but was fatally wounded while returning to his platoon.

As a boy, he had had a particular fondness for the largest of the quarries opened by the London Granite Company, and this was the place chosen by his family for his memorial. An inscription, on a four-foot high slab of blue Oxfordshire gault, set in granite, records his death of wounds on April 9th, 1944, and the award of the Victoria Cross. It begins 'Greater love hath no man than this, that a man lay down his life for his friends' and ends 'At the going down of the sun and in the morning we will remember them'.

On a day of warm midsummer sunshine the Vicar of Appledore, the Rev. Muller, conducted a service in the quarry, attended by members of the Harman family, friends and representatives of John Harman's regiment, the coastguard service and Trinity House. Rear-Admiral Franklin, who had been in command at Appledore during the war, was also present. The memorial may be seen by any visitor to Lundy who cares to walk to 'V.C. Quarry'.

In 1946 a group of naturalists headed by Professor L.A. Harvey of the Department of Zoology of Exeter University sought and obtained Martin Harman's approval for the setting up of a Lundy Field Society. He had a keen interest in natural history and a life-long love of the countryside; one of his reasons for buying Lundy had been to keep it as 'a remote, wild and primitive island where wildlife predominated and all lived in peace and seclusion'. He offered the use of the Old Light, rent free, as the Society's

Plate 9

Felix Gade on the Landing Beach

headquarters, the only stipulation being that any repairs that might become necessary would be carried out by the Society.

The objects of the Society were, and are, 'to further the study of the birds of Lundy and in particular their migration and movements; to undertake biological investigations of the wild life of the island; to further the conservation of the fauna and flora of the island'. A Warden was appointed, Heligoland traps were set up (sometimes needing replacement because of weather damage) so that a programme of bird ringing could be undertaken, and members of the Society and students visited the island at fairly frequent intervals to work on special study projects, the results usually being published in the Society's annual reports, which appeared in the form of sixty to seventy-page booklets.

Martin Harman accepted the invitation to become President, and took a close interest — not always approving — in the Society's activities. For the second annual report, in 1948, he wrote a 'President's Letter', but in the next five years, until his death, the heading was changed to 'Owner's Letter'. He sometimes suggested work the Society might undertake, or offered criticism or congratulation.

It occurred to him that the twelve-mile crossing from Hartland to Lundy might offer a challenge to swimmers comparable to the more usual Channel swim, and offered a prize to the first person to achieve this. An Egyptian, Captain Abdul-el-Rehim, who had already swam the English Channel four times, and in 1952 held the record of 10 hours 52 minutes, decided to try the Lundy swim. It took him about 12 hours to complete it. 'The North Devon Journal-Herald' of August 7th, 1952, quoted him as saying that he found it more difficult than the Channel. Having once stepped ashore on the island, he did not linger, but returned to the mainland immediately in his escort boat.

The return of Felix Gade to Lundy was appreciated by the Society; according to Professor Harvey, he had 'infused new life into the island, re-opening the Marisco Stores, improving the *Lerina's* sailing schedules and establishing friendly and confident relations with the Society'.

However, although the *Lerina* had been bought back from the Admiralty in 1946, her years of war service had almost worn her out; what was worse, she had been lying at a mooring on the Torridge for two years, and was in a weakened state, not improved when she grounded on the landing beach during a windy night at Christmas, 1947. Although she carried passengers and stores to and from the island for another three years, repeated and increasingly expensive trouble with her engine sometimes caused her to be out of service, and she was finally laid up in 1950. (She was eventually sold by public auction for the derisory sum of one pound, to Percy Eastman, a shipbreaker of Appledore, in 1955.)

In summer, both day trippers and those wanting to spend longer on the island could cross on the Campbell steamers, which were also prepared to transport supplies, but from late September to early May there was no regular vessel to serve the island. A boat called the *Annie Vesta* was sometimes chartered, and George Irwin of Ilfracombe was often willing to make the crossing in his trawler *Girl Joyce*; Lundy Field Society members usually sailed with him.

Fortunately those living on Lundy were not wholly dependent on sea-borne transport during these years. In 1950 a former RAF pilot named Drabble made arrangements with the Air Ministry to rent premises on the RAF station at Chivenor, and was granted the right to take off and land on the airfield at times agreed with the officer on duty. Plans were made to restart the prewar air service of passengers, freight and mail, and Lundy's old runways were cleared and extended to meet Air Ministry requirements. A company called Devon Air Travel Ltd. was formed to operate from Chivenor, and Felix Gade was appointed to its board of directors as Martin Harman's nominee.

The aircraft used was a De Havilland Rapide, a twin-engined biplane. It seated six passengers, but the seats could be removed when stores were being carried. The venture was short-lived; after two years the Rapide was repossessed and Mr. Drabble was compelled to wind up the company. However, a new company, Devonair Ltd., was formed by another ex-RAF pilot, Maurice

Looker, flying Austers. In August, 1955, as he was flying over Barnstaple Bay on his way to the mainland with passengers, his engine cut out. He landed on the water and a nearby ship picked up pilot and passengers unharmed, and carried them to South Wales. At the resulting Air Ministry enquiry it was decreed that no commercial flying might be undertaken except in particularly fine weather. Although Maurice Looker made a few more flights to Lundy between the autumn of 1955 and the spring of 1956, the accident meant that there was little prospect of a future for Devonair Ltd., especially when it became clear that Lundy was soon to acquire a supply vessel of its own once more.

The reintroduction of air mail to Lundy had prompted Martin Harman to re-issue stamps in denominations of half puffin to twelve puffin overprinted BY AIR, and to commission John Dyke, a talented local artist, to design seven new stamps, each one showing a seabird in flight. The half puffin was still, literally, a puffin; the other birds depicted were the guillemot, kittiwake, razorbill, fulmar, oyster catcher and greater black-backed gull. Puffinage rates were increased, although a letter of less than two ounces still went for a half puffin.

It had been intended to issue a specially designed stamp to celebrate the coronation of Elizabeth II in 1953, but a decision about the design was left too late, and only an over-printing 'Coronation 2.6.53' was made on existing stamps.

In 1954 it was decided to commemorate the silver jubilee of the very first Lundy stamps by producing sets of both surface and airmail stamps. The artist was again John Dyke; he produced fourteen excellent designs. Those for surface mail showed five different places on Lundy, a map of the island, and the much-lamented *Lerina;* those for air mail depicted historic aircraft, from a hot air balloon of 1850 to the Bristol Brabazon.

In December, 1954, Martin Harman died suddenly of a heart attack. In tributes to him which appeared in the Lundy Field Society's annual report, a friend whose meetings with him had been largely confined to the City wrote that 'simple and unostentatious in the way he lived, yet lavishly generous to those he liked, self-confident yet without any self-conceit, with a love of nature and a capacity for friendship with people of every type, and with a sense of humour that did not spare himself, he was quite unlike the popular idea of a financier'. Professor Harvey spoke of his vigour and vision; it was due to his help and encouragement that the Society had succeeded, and its debt to him was beyond telling; he had been 'an everlasting source of delight and strength'. Felix Gade wrote of his deep grief at the death of the man he had known and admired for so long.

Ownership of the island passed to his surviving children, Albion, Diana and Ruth. All three were married, with families, and had commitments on the mainland; they all visited Lundy when they could but, like their father, they did not live there. Continuity in the management of island affairs was assured by the presence of Felix Gade, whose knowledge and experience could not be equalled by any other islander.

The perennial problem remained of ensuring that the island continued to pay its way and even earn a modest profit. One way of doing this was to increase the number of holiday lettings. A building originally known as the Cable Hut, constructed by the Post Office against the north-east wall of the Castle Keep in the 1890s as the terminal of the cable to Croyde, was enlarged, renovated and renamed Castle Cottage. A dwelling once called Cliff Bungalow, built in 1902 by a fisherman named George Thomas, had come to be known as Hanmers, after a family who stayed there often in the 1930s; this was also improved and refurnished. The Old Light offered hostel-type accommodation: fourteen beds in eight rooms for groups who had no objection to fairly spartan conditions. A new tea garden was opened to cater for the hundreds of day visitors who arrived on the pleasure steamers in summer.

The intermittent difficulty in communication with the mainland that had been experienced for six years ended in June, 1956, with the arrival of a former Scottish fishing boat, the *Pride of Bridlington*, built in 1950. Albion Harman had bought her after searching for some time for a suitable supply boat. She was to have been named *Gannet*, after Captain William Dark's long-lived cutter, but permission was refused, as there was already a *Gannet* on the register of shipping. Albion Harman's son John, named after his heroic uncle, suggested that she should be called the *Lundy Gannet*, and this was accepted. Her arrival, celebrated by the despatch of 500 first day covers bearing the words 'Maiden Voyage of the *Lundy Gannet*' caused rejoicing, not only among islanders but among members of the Lundy Field Society: that year, for the first time, the Old Light hostel showed a credit balance.

On the death of his father, Albion Harman had accepted the invitation to succeed him as president of the Society; from 1954 to 1957 he wrote an 'Owner's letter'. In the 1956 letter he declared his intention to make the island 'a little less of a zoo and more of a farm'. In pursuit of this aim he ordered a radical reduction of the numbers of animals on the island.

Lundy ponies had multiplied during the war, when no transport was available to take surplus numbers to the mainland for sale. However, on the orders of Martin Harman, some fifty had been sent away — mostly for slaughter — in 1949. In view of his reputed concern for animals it is surprising that he should not have tried to ensure that they went to private buyers as riding ponies. Instead they were hauled roughly aboard the *Lerina* on rope slings and landed on Bideford Quay by the same method, which caused some onlookers to write to the local press and the RSPCA. To be driven from the freedom of the wild, peaceful island, subjected to the fright and discomfort of being shipped to the mainland, by road to the noise and bewilderment of Barnstaple cattle market and, finally, to the abattoir, was a harsh ending to their lives.

In 1952 and 1953 Martin Harman, accompanied by some officers of the regiment in which his son had served, had carried out a limited cull of deer and goats. After this he estimated that some 130 deer remained, which he considered the optimum population. He seems to have had no intention of killing any of the Soay sheep he had introduced, or the wild goats; in his 1948 letter he observed that neither species was increasing as he had hoped. His son had a different view. He employed a man named Charlie Collins, who had had considerable experiences of shooting red deer in his native New Zealand, to begin a wholesale slaughter. Fallow deer were already extinct on the island; the herd had dwindled away by 1954 as the result of the activities of Van Os early in the war. Red deer too had been killed by visiting 'sportsmen' in considerable numbers. Using a .303 rifle, Collins shot 38 Soay sheep, 28 goats and 86 deer in a fortnight in January, 1957, and in October of the same year shot a further 78 Soay sheep, 4 goats and 45 deer. Having done this, he estimated that there were still 12 sheep, 30 deer and 27 goats on the island. As a result, the red deer became extinct by 1962. Only the prudently shy Sika, which hid themselves in dense rhododendron thickets clothing the sidelands on the east side of the island, managed to remain in sufficient numbers to form a viable herd.

Interest in Lundy stamps among philatelists in many parts of the world — first shown in the Thirties and continued, somewhat surprisingly, during the war — ensured that new issues, together with first-day covers, were profitable. Three years after Martin Harman's death there was a definitive re-issue of the last set of stamps he had planned. These had been intended to celebrate the thousandth anniversary of the unification of England under one king, following the death of Erik Bloodaxe, king of Northumbria, in 954: a perhaps characteristically idiosyncratic choice. For surface mail a London artist named Ilett produced six designs depicting Lundy ponies and one showing Erik Bloodaxe with a Viking ship. In each of the seven airmail stamps a bird was the subject, all species to be seen on Lundy — buzzard, cormorant, Manx Shearwater, lapwing, ring ousel and, as in John Dyke's 1950 designs, a fulmar and a puffin, although this time the puffin was seen alongside Erik Bloodaxe.

The set of seven Lundy pony designs which had appeared in 1955, overprinted EUROPA and with the colours of the denominations changed, was re-issued in 1961 to celebrate the second anniversary of the Conference of European Posts and Communications. The following year Albion Harman decided to support the

World Health Organisation's anti-malarial campaign by issuing a set of six diamond-shaped stamps; five showed Lundy scenes, but the sixth depicted an anopheles mosquito. He had business interests in west Africa, and as a result of visits there was himself a malaria sufferer.

The 400th anniversary of Shakespeare's birth, in 1964, was celebrated by an impressive stamp designed by C. F. Tunnicliffe and issued in three denominations: it portrayed a bust of the poet and a peregrine falcon, with the quotation 'A falcon towering over her pride of place'. The next year, following the death of Sir Winston Churchill, a stamp was brought out which might have been taken as implying that he had some connection with Lundy: it showed him in the uniform of the Elder Brethren of Trinity House, gazing over Lametor towards the Devon coast. The wreck of the *Torrey Canyon* on the Seven Stones reef in March, 1967, and the consequent loss of life among seabirds, prompted Albion Harman to commission Tunnicliffe to design a stamp which he hoped would raise money for both the RSPBA and the International Society for the Protection of Animals. It showed a group of puffins resting on a clump of sea thrift, with a tanker in the distance, and bore the words 'Help Save Seabirds from oil' in English, French, Dutch and German. Unfortunately too large a printing was ordered, and large quantities of these stamps remained unsold.

Not long after this Albion Harman's health began to fail. On a visit to Lundy in June, 1967, he died of a heart attack in a helicopter carrying him to hospital. His ashes were brought back to the island and buried under a granite cairn near the grave of his parents.

His widow and his two sisters were now the owners of Lundy, but within a few months had made the decision that the island must be put up for sale. Many people felt dismayed at the news. Who would buy it? What would they do with it? Would it be commercialized, and lose its character?

Discounting the brief interlude of Augustus Christie's ownership, for nearly 130 years Lundy had been loved and cared for by just two families, who had done their best to ensure that it changed as little as possible. Was there anyone who would be willing to follow their example?

Chapter Thirteen

In the months that followed the announcement in March, 1969, that Lundy was for sale, many people appeared to be thinking of buying it.[1] Many more were concerned about its future, and considered that the ideal buyer would be the National Trust. As Lundy forms part of the Torridge constituency, Peter (now Sir Peter) Mills, M.P. for that constituency, took practical action. He was reported as fearing that the island might 'fall into the hands of someone who would use it in a totally unscrupulous way for commercial exploitation'.[2] He had hopes that the Ministry of Housing and Local Government might provide a grant to make it possible for the National Trust to buy Lundy, but as this was not forthcoming he discussed the problem with Jeremy Thorpe, then M.P. for North Devon, and David Owen (now Lord Owen) M.P. for Sutton, Plymouth, who gave him their wholehearted support to launch an appeal for enough money to ensure that the Trust could at least make an offer for the island. Jeremy Thorpe was especially active in his efforts to publicize the appeal. It was proposed that subscribers, to be known as 'Founder Friends of Lundy' should make donations of £25 each. Within three months, over £30,000 had been raised, but it was far below the amount needed.

The Harman family decided to put the island up for auction in June — later postponing this to July. Suddenly, well before the date set, a rescuer appeared. The front page of the 'North Devon Journal-Herald' (as it then was) for 29th May, 1969, bore a large aerial photograph of the south end of Lundy with a bold headline, 'Lundy Safe for All Time', and announced that Jack Hayward, a Bahamas businessman aged 46, from Sussex, known as 'Union Jack' because of his pride in Britain, had made an offer of £150,000 in order that the island might indeed become the property of the National Trust. The Harman family accepted. and thousands of people felt relief and joy in the knowledge that the island could remain a place of wildness and quietude.

(Nevertheless, care was taken that the island's status was clearly defined; the 'Western Morning News' for May 16th, 1969, had already reported that conditions of sale included agreement that Lundy 'must be regarded as under the dominion of the Crown, and any reference to or the fact of the non-levy of rates or taxes, or non-enforcement of licensing laws, must not be taken as intended to imply that the Crown and those exercising authority under the Crown disclaim jurisdiction, fiscal or otherwise'. In consequence, the islanders have since had to pay income tax and the short-lived poll tax, and will be liable for whatever changes in rating may follow.)

The Landmark Trust, having leased the island for a period of sixty years, took over its management. Felix Gade, who may be seen as the Grand Old Man of Lundy — he was by this time 79 years old — continued as agent during the period of transition.

On Sunday, September 28th, 1969, a service of thanksgiving was held in the church of St. Helena. Campbells made two ships available, the *Westward Ho!* and the *St. Trillo*, and more than a thousand lovers of Lundy crossed to attend. The church could not, of course, accommodate such a huge congregation, and the service, conducted by the Bishop of Crediton, the Right Rev. Wilfred Westall, was relayed by loudspeakers to listeners outside.

Jack (now Sir Jack) Hayward who, before making his remarkable philanthropic gesture, had never so much as seen Lundy, was present as guest of honour. He was visiting the island for the second time: on July 6th, at a special ceremony outside the Marisco Tavern, attended by two of the promoters of the Lundy Appeal, Peter Mills and Jeremy Thorpe, and the chairman of the National Trust, the Earl of Antrim, Felix Gade presented Mr. Hayward with an illuminated vellum scroll, decorated in gold leaf. It bore drawings by John Dyke, in Indian ink, of Lundy features such as the Knight Templar rock, the Castle and the Old Light. Flanking an inscription were two mythical figures: Drayton's personification of Lundy as a 'lusty black-browed girl' and a portrayal of Neptune with the slogan originated by Martin Harman, ' Lundy Lights and Leads' below it.

The inscription read:

'To Jack Hayward, Esq., O.B.E.

We the islanders of Lundy whose names appear below desire to thank you from the bottom of our hearts for your great act of spontaneous generosity in providing the National Trust with the money to purchase Lundy, thus preserving this beautiful unspoilt island for all time.

Not only we who live here honour and thank you, but many thousands of people who delight in visiting Lundy to enjoy its peace and freedom from the stresses of modern life, join us in acclaiming you as a warm-hearted and far-sighted benefactor.'[3]

Another presentation made at the same time, by the two M.P.s, was a bound volume of coloured views of the island.

John Dyke's increasing interest in the life of Lundy led to his moving there to live early in 1970. With his wife he settled into a cottage near the Marisco Castle, and at once began work, collecting exhibits for the museum then planned and, perhaps more importantly, preparing the first issue of the 'Illustrated Lundy News and Landmark Journal'. The fact that the title echoed that of a long-established magazine was wittily emphasized by the cover heading: in the style of the 'Illustrated London News', John Dyke produced a view of Lundy outlined on the horizon, with sailing ships and an expanse of sea in the foreground. Below appeared a drawing of the South Light and Rat Island seen from Hangman's Hill, on which the Union Jack and the Lundy flag were shown together on a tall flagpole, as they were on September 28th, 1969.

He prefaced this issue with a brief editorial in which, after making mention of the 'Cave and Lundy Review' of early 19th century Barnstaple, he paid tribute to a very much more recent publication. The editor of this was Stanley Smith, who had first arrived on Lundy in 1931, as a youth of seventeen, to work in the Manor Farm Hotel kitchen. Later he took over the running of the Marisco Tavern and Stores. Having married in 1938, he served in the Royal Army Ordnance Corps during the war, and afterwards returned to his home in Skewen, Glamorgan. He and his family spent holidays on Lundy, and in 1956 arrived to live there again. He had contracted to be responsible for the necessary maintenance and repair work, and to serve in the Tavern in the evenings, while his wife ran the Stores. Three years later they returned to the mainland to take over the Blacksmiths Arms in Bideford, but between the spring of 1957 and the winter of 1960-61 Stanley Smith brought out six issues of his magazine, the 'Lundy Review' which, as John Dyke observed, 'presented an astonishing number of interesting features from writers well known for their close association with Lundy'. The second issue contained an account of a brief private and informal visit paid by the Queen Mother in May, 1958, on her way back from an official function in Belfast, aboard *Britannia*. No publicity at all was given to this. The Queen Mother disembarked from the *Britannia's* pinnace on a sunny afternoon, and declined the offer of a ride up the beach road in a specially prepared trailer with the splendidly characteristic remark 'Oh no! I shall walk. You must not forget that I am a Scotswoman, and can walk'.[4] After visiting the church, Millcombe House and the Marisco Stores, she and her entourage enjoyed a picnic tea in a sheltered place near the drive gates of Millcombe.

Included in the first issue of the 'Illustrated Lundy News' was a message from John Smith, founder and chairman of the Landmark Trust, in which he said 'The purpose of this magazine — for which we are *exceedingly* lucky to have John Dyke as editor — is to bind Lundy and its admirers together. Lundy is a world apart — and a fairly secret world at that. Those who find it and are "hooked" by it have ever after something special in common with each other — be they bird-watchers, archaeologists, botanists, climbers, divers, lovers of solitude, or lovers of good company'. He considered that Lundy should seek to offer nothing but itself, rather than things that could be got elsewhere or that would endanger its qualities of simplicity and tranquillity. He wanted it to be a going concern all the year round, with genuine jobs and livelihoods for everybody, and recognized that this would mean a lot of capital expenditure.

From an editorial address as unique as the magazine produced in it — Signal Cottage, Lundy, Bristol Channel, via Ilfracombe, North Devon — in other words the cottage he was living in, John Dyke published, at intervals of three or four months over the next five years, fifteen issues. Every cover design was his work; he enhanced and enlivened page after page of the text with drawings. He even illustrated advertisements. The back cover of the first ten issues bore a drawing by him of passengers landing from a pleasure steamer by the launch *Devonia*; this announced 'sailings to Lundy Island throughout the summer season by the White Funnel Fleet'. Others drew attention to the Manor House Hotel, to holiday lettings in cottages on the island, and to all-the-year-round sailings from Ilfracombe aboard the *Lundy Gannet*.

Each issue also contained many photographs of people, animals and events on Lundy; most were contemporary, although a few have a particular interest because they date back to the late 19th or early 20th century.

A feature that appeared in every issue was 'Lundy Log', which was exactly that: a daily record of weather, arrivals and departures of ships and some of their passengers, names of vessels taking shelter in Lundy Roads, notes on farm and building work, and observations of birds, either resident or migrant. Other recurring items were 'This made News' — reports concerning Lundy drawn from newspapers fifty, seventy-five or a hundred years earlier — and, following Stanley Smith's example in the 'Lundy Review', extracts from Philip Gosse's SEA AND LAND. There were a number of articles by Barry Chinchen on the history of Lundy stamps, and by various writers on some of the pleasure steamers that had served the Lundy run. Of particular interest are articles by Myrtle Langham, one on William Hudson Heaven and two on 'Lundy a Hundred Years Ago', drawn from information supplied by Miss Eileen Heaven, his great-granddaughter. Miss Heaven herself contributed 'On Rowing Round the Island: an Edwardian Recollection'. She recalled doing this twice, with three or four companions in what she describes as a twelve foot punt. On one of these excursions the oarsmen took the boat through the tunnel-like cave at the north-west point, and the passengers 'watched the fresh water of the Virgin's Spring bubbling up through the salt' — a phenomenon that some writers appear to have doubted.

Despite difficulties such as the postal strike of 1971, and the illness of the editor necessitating an emergency helicopter flight to hospital in Bideford, the magazine continued to appear until, in 1975, the fifteenth issue contained a message from John Smith. 'This will, sadly, be the last issue of the 'Illustrated Lundy News' in its present form. It is now more uneconomic than ever to produce and, as there is constant pressure to reduce our costs, we have reluctantly decided to give it up'. He also announced that the building work necessary to open the projected museum would also have to be put off for two or three years. John Dyke was to move to Boscastle to do more designing work for the National Trust, as he had done before arriving on Lundy.

Yet although it was short-lived, the magazine's many line drawings, its photographs and Lundy Log provide a splendid account of the island's life during the first five years under the Landmark Trust's management, and its other contents are full of interest for anyone who loves the island.

(In the mid-1980s a new publication, the 'Lundy Island Chronicle' began to appear. Edited by Wendy Puddy, it contained articles, photographs and occasional drawings all relating to life on the island. Several issues were produced during the next four years, but unfortunately by 1988 this too had fallen victim to the ever-increasing cost of printing.)

Felix Cade celebrated his 80th birthday in July 1970, (A cricket match between 'F. W. Gade's Eleven and the Gentlemen of Wessex' was played in his honour, and the islanders presented him with a barometer.) The following year — possibly with reluctance — he acknowledged that he was 'not the man that was needed, and that I am now too old to carry out all the duties fully',[8] and resigned. He was succeeded by Ian Grainger, who had come to Lundy not long before as resident engineer and assistant agent. (When Ian Grainger left in 1979, his successor was Robert Gilliatt, who in turn was followed in 1983 by the Landmark Trust's present agent, John Puddy).

On October 1st, 1971, following Mr. Gade's last day as agent, a party was held in the Marisco Tavern, with some forty guests, including his two daughters and three grandchildren and eight members of the Harman family. John Smith made a speech in praise of his remarkable career in the service of Lundy, ending with the words 'And he retires, like an Admiral of the Fleet, on full pay'.[6]

Felix Gade continued to live on the island, in accommodation provided by the Landmark Trust, for the last seven years of his life, first occupying himself with the philatelic side of Lundy's business, including two new stamp issues in 1972, and later, after the death of his wife in 1973, with the writing of his autobiography, MY LIFE ON LUNDY. Its almost defiant opening sentence runs: 'I am Felix William Gade, aged ei /-five years old, and I have lived on Lundy, in the Bristol Channel, for fifty years; my wife, Edith Irene Gade, lived on Lundy for just on thirty-six years'.

Although he had started to put together his recollections more than a decade earlier, he might have gone on with them during the sad years of his widowhood but for the help and encouragement which, as he acknowledged, he had received from Myrtle Langham, the co-author, with her husband, of LUNDY, BRISTOL CHANNEL.[7] His book was published privately in the year he died. His death broke the last link with the Lundy of the 1920s and 1930s, when Martin Coles Harman strove to maintain Lundy's autonomy against all comers; when the majestic paddle steamers of the White Funnel Fleet ploughed the broad white furrows of their wakes out of Ilfracombe harbour and across Barnstaple Bay throughout the summer months; and when the *Lerina*, captained by Fred Dark, sailed all the year round, whenever weather conditions made it at all possible, to serve the island's people.

The national census of April, 1971, showed that Lundy had twenty-eight inhabitants and seasonal workers, five hotel guests, four visitors in cottage lettings and six campers.[8] The second and third issues of the 'Illustrated Lundy News' had carried advertisements for 'experienced tradesmen to take part in the extensive repair, restoration and rebuilding works now to be undertaken on Lundy and expected to last some six years'; however, the first need was for a dwelling for Ian Grainger and his family, and this was a cedar structure erected to replace an old corrugated iron building known as Bramble Villa.

An early job was the stabilizing of the beach road, which had seen a number of landslides since the war. The most recent had been in February, 1969, and although repairs had been made remarkably quickly, using gabions, more needed to be done. In 1971 scaffolding went up around Millcombe House. By the following summer it had been restored internally and given a new copper roof. A row of timber dwellings for the building workers was being built in the area engagingly known as Pig's Paradise. (Named at that time Paradise Row, it was later converted for use as holiday lettings and is now called the Quarters.) Within eight or nine years the Manor House Hotel, the Castle and the church were restored, and the barn once intended to house the museum was given a new roof and made ready for use as a hostel, providing fourteen beds. Felix Gade, invited to declare it open in 1975, remembered 'all the work which had been carried out there when it was a farm building; threshing, chaff-cutting, cake-crushing, sawing timber, grinding oats, shearing', using an old Blackstone oil engine which was difficult to start.

The 75th anniversary of the consecration of St. Helena's church was celebrated on June 7th, 1972, with a service conducted by the priest in charge of Lundy, the Rev. Dixon. Residents and visitors attended, and the first lesson was read by Miss Eileen Heaven, great niece of the Rev. Hudson Heaven, by this time 79 years old. In 1969 she had made a donation of seven thousand pounds towards the restoration of the church. A set of five stamps designed by John Dyke was issued to mark the event, showing views of the church both inside and out, and a portrait of the Rev. Heaven. (A second stamp issue that year commemorated the completion of the North and South Lighthouses in 1897.)

The following August Lundy had its first royal visit since 1958:

the Duke and Duchess of Kent, accompanied by their children, were spending a holiday in the Putsborough area, and attended RAF Chivenor's International Air Day. A few days later the Duke and his family, together with Jeremy Thorpe and his son Rupert, arrived on the island aboard a small vessel, the *Lundy Puffin*. All the children had rides on Lundy ponies, of which there was still a reasonably sized herd. (A short time after this, recognition of the Lundy pony as a specific breed was given by the National Pony Society — somewhat ironically, as over the next decade or so their numbers were allowed to decline. In 1979 there were ten mares, a stallion and eight foals; [9] by 1990 only three aging mares remained on the island, although fortunately there were others living on the mainland. An effort is being made to re-establish a small island herd.)

During the 1980s the Lundy Field Society had been in financial difficulties, but in 1971 it chartered the M.V. *Balmoral* for a well-advertised excursion to the island which produced a handsome profit. From then on similar trips were run annually, and the Society's funds benefited to such an extent that it was able to offer grants to undergraduates and graduates to carry out field work on a variety of aspects of the island's wildlife.

Membership increased gradually from the original total to over 500. The Landmark Trust offered to finance the appointment of a Warden for the Society, who was to live in the Old Light. However the young man appointed married the following year and, as married quarters were not available, left at the end of 1973. An accredited bird ringer who worked on the island acted as unofficial bird observer and made daily recordings until he left in 1978.

A number of members of the Society were in favour of trying to establish Lundy as a marine nature reserve. An article by Keith Hiscock in the 'Illustrated Lundy News' in the summer of 1971, illustrated with photographs, described the 'amazingly rich and colourful fauna' in the seas immediately around the island, and outlined the proposal to ensure its conservation. He warned that much work lay ahead before a marine nature reserve could be formally designated. His warning was justified. Although the

Landmark Trust approved the proposal in principle, and the island indeed became a voluntary nature reserve in 1973, it was not until November, 1986, that William Waldegrave, then Minister for the Environment, made a formal announcement that Lundy had been designated Britain's first marine nature reserve. Shortly afterwards Anglia Television made a film on Lundy's underwater life for their Survival series, making it possible for millions of viewers to see an aspect of the island that until the second half of the twentieth century was almost unknown, and even today can only be explored fully by those who have trained as divers: the many-coloured submarine garden of sea anemones, corals and sponges flourishing deep in the clear water.

For the moment, the status of marine nature reserve gives the island's coast some protection — yet it is a fragile one. In a world that has decided to make oil its economic lifeblood, no part of any ocean can truly be protected while all are crossed and recrossed by loaded tankers always at risk from collision or wreck. There is, too, the tireless search for offshore oil. In August, 1992, it was announced that new licences for exploration in Britain's western waters would be available, and it was thought possible that one site might be within only a few miles of Lundy.

Although for centuries it was taken for granted that the wild creatures on and around the island — birds, seals, fish — were the legitimate prey of human beings for livelihood or sport, until recently species were sufficiently resilient to withstand losses. They might be attacked; their habitat was not. Today, when the threat is universal, well-meaning statutes offer only the flimsiest of shields.

Chapter Fourteen

In July, 1971, a small ship formerly in the service of the Royal Greenland Company anchored for a few hours in Lundy Roads, and the islanders viewed her with interest. She had been the *Agdleq*, but she bore on her bows the emblem of her previous owners, and from this she received her English name: the *Polar Bear*. She had been bought by the Landmark Trust as the island's new supply ship. She was 149 feet long, had cabin berths for ten passengers and accommodation for a crew of seven. She was provided with a range of navigational aids and, having two powerful hydraulic winches, could handle considerably heavier cargo than the *Lundy Gannet,* although the latter continued to carry some stores, as well as passengers.

The sturdy little *Polar Bear* was to serve Lundy for fourteen years. Originally based at Ilfracombe, she was moved to Bideford in 1983, despite strenuous objections by Ilfracombe Council and traders. The fact that, like the *Lundy Puffin*, she could carry only a few passengers was unimportant as long as the pleasure steamers continued to run each summer, bringing hundreds of day trippers to the island every week. Yet as early as the 1950s there had been signs of difficulties ahead: after several poor seasons the firm of P and A. Campbell had been struggling to survive. In 1959 their company became a subsidiary of George Nott Industries, which owned Townsend Ferries, although their name, and that of the White Funnel Fleet, were retained.

Nevertheless, the day of the paddle steamer was almost over. The *Britannia* was scrapped at Newport in 1960, the *Glen Usk*, the *Glen Gower*, the *Cardiff Queen* and the *Bristol Queen* were all scrapped between 1960 and 1968. From 1969 just one excursion steamer, the

M.V. *Balmoral*, was visiting Lundy. (She could, and still can, carry more than 700 passengers.) At the end of the 1970s she was withdrawn, and in her place the *Prince Ivanhoe*, for a short time, operated trips in the Bristol Channel until in May, 1981, she ran aground off the Welsh coast. As a result, both Ilfracombe and Lundy faced a sharp drop in revenue during that summer, and for the foreseeable future.

There was still one ocean-going paddle steamer in a serviceable condition: the *Waverley*. A number of people had become so alarmed at the steady destruction of the much-loved paddlers that in the late 1960s they had formed the Paddle Steamer Preservation Society — which in due course became a registered charity — to buy one or two of those that remained and restore them to a seaworthy, passenger-carrying condition, and the *Waverley* became their most splendid acquisition. She was based at first in Scotland, but began to make occasional summer voyages south to call at Ilfracombe and enable holiday-makers to visit Lundy once more.

Such visits were too infrequent to solve Lundy's problems. In the spring of 1981 the Landmark Trust made arrangements for a Liskeard firm, Castle Air Charters, to run a helicopter service from a landing place behind the coastguard station at Hartland Point to Lundy. Air fares were considerably higher than boat fares, and only a few passengers could cross at one time; however, for those who were prepared to pay the price, the great advantage was the speed of the crossing: some seven minutes, instead of a steamer's two hours or so.

In 1985 the Civil Aviation Authority imposed very strict regulations regarding the use of helicopters over the sea. This meant that already high fares might have to be doubled. The Landmark Trust decided that it was time for Lundy to have a ship of its own capable of carrying large numbers of passengers as well as freight. The English Tourist Board made a grant of £70,000 towards the cost of buying such a ship.

After several months, the search for a suitable vessel ended with the discovery of the 300 ton *Oldenburg* in Germany. Sailing from

Wilhelmshaven in December, 1985, she called briefly at Lundy before continuing her voyage to Bideford for a refit. She came into service in May, 1986, just five years after the accident to the *Prince Ivanhoe*. She can carry twenty tons of cargo and more than 260 passengers.

The Paddle Steamer Preservation Society had meanwhile bought the *Balmoral* and restored her to her old splendour as a pleasure steamer visiting Ilfracombe, Lynmouth and Lundy. Once more, the island was able to welcome many thousand day visitors every year, as well as those who arrived to stay in the increased number of holiday lettings for a week or more.

Ilfracombe harbour:the *Oldenburg* at the pier. On her squat funnel is a black and white picture of a puffin; banners along her sides announce cruises to Lundy. A rainy August has merged into a rainy early September, with strong Atlantic winds pushing a full tide into the mouth of the Bristol Channel. Yet a small crowd is waiting at the pier. A few have luggage, so are going to stay on Lundy, but many more are evidently holiday-makers going over for the day, in spite of the weather.

Using the ships own crane, cargo is loaded into the hold under the forward deck. Once the hatches are replaced and the crane has been telescoped down into itself, a gangway is hauled into place, and it is time to duck out of the rain and choose somewhere to shelter. An awning covers the seats on the after deck, but on a day like this the warmth of the buffet or bar seems preferable.

Inevitably it is an uncomfortable crossing on a lumpy sea, and probably few people enjoy it. Yet it lasts only about two and a half hours, and we are all warm and dry. What was it like in the days of sail, when visitors like Philip Gosse endured a voyage lasting many hours in an open boat, sitting in clothes soaked by spray or a wave over the bows almost as soon as they set out?

Lundy grows larger out of rain squalls. The sea quietens, the ship eases into her anchorage in the lee of Rat Island, and a launch comes out to carry the first thirty people ashore. In a few minutes the

Plate 10

The inner bar (formerly Marisco Cottage) of the Marisco Tavern

silvery shingle of the beach is crunching underfoot. It may surprise some first-time visitors to land on what they have understood to be a granite island and find themselves on a slaty shore, with pale slate cliffs rising above it. Yet it is this friable slate of the island's southern tip, yielding to the sea, that has for centuries offered seafarers a landing place.

A new road has been cut round to the Cove, where a diving centre is based. The lower part of the old way up to the South Light fell in a storm a few years ago; the steps break off in mid-air, and a length of handrail overhangs a steep scree. Flights of new concrete steps and a zigzag path lead up to the lighthouse entrance, with its notice announcing that a sudden loud blast of the foghorn may be sounded at any time without warning. It is still a manned light, but it will soon be automated, as the North Light already is.

Above the new road, rows of huge studs mark the ends of iron rods driven into the sheer rock wall in an attempt to stabilize them, yet the cutting still looks precarious. It is this tendency of the slate to shatter that has caused recurrent landslides on the track up from the landing beach. (One, in 1954, demolished the limekiln that used to stand on the quay.) The last was in 1979, when a large fall left a deep cleft, and a west country newspaper carried an alarmist headline, 'Lundy May be Abandoned'. It was reported that Group Captain W. R. Williams, secretary to the Landmark Trust, had written to Torridge District Council to say that unless the necessary work was done, the island could not be serviced. 'The work required will be extremely expensive and consequently, in the absence of financial help the Trust must now consider removing the population and abandoning the island.'

Financial help was provided, repairs were made, and today the *Oldenburg's* passengers, like the thousands who visit Lundy every year, can climb the steep winding track to the village without seeing any sign of damage.

Here and there alongside the track grows an unremarkable-looking plant: it is the Lundy Cabbage, first noted by a doctor-naturalist, Frederick Elliston Wright, who practised for many years in Braunton and was acknowledged by Henry Williamson as his mentor in all to do with the plants of the north Devon countryside, especially Braunton Burrows. Originally classified as *Brassicella Wrightii*, it is now known as *Rynchosinapsis Wrightii*, and apparently grows nowhere else but on Lundy.

The road curves west into Millcombe. It is a long time since a mill stood in this valley, but the stream that worked it trickles through a silted-up marshy bed that was the mill pond. On either side of the road are grassy spaces, each with a seat: one 'In memory of Betty Hindon who loved Lundy' and the other presented by the W.I. Lundy Group to commemorate the Devon Federation of Women's Institutes' Golden Jubilee in 1970. To the north rises Hangman's Hill, with its flagstaff and the little shelter built by the Heaven family and known as the Ugly.

A sharp hairpin bend takes one up St. John's Valley and past the church to the village, but walkers pass the three walled kitchen gardens that once grew vegetables for The Villa and take a path through the grounds of the house built when William IV's reign was about to merge into Victoria's, but hailing back to a plain late Georgian style. The path winds upwards until one can look down on its restored copper roof. At this point is a third seat, in a recess, with a plaque inscribed:

'In memory of Albion P. Harman, joint overlord of Lundy 1954-1968, a collection of trees and shrubs was planted in Millcombe by the Lundy Field Society and other friends, 1970.'

Although trees cannot tolerate the weather on the high tableland of Lundy, in this valley, and to some extent on the eastern sidelands, sycamore and Turkey oak, ash, willow and even aspen can survive.

A last steep slope, a flight of steps, and a small gate leads into pasture where many sheep graze, indifferent to the familiar sight of wandering human beings. In the adjoining St. Helen's field are a dozen cattle — and three ponies. Are there others on the island, or did the attempt, a few years ago, to revive the island's herd not succeed? I look forward to finding out.

The village is small enough, certainly, but distinguished as a village rather than a hamlet because it has a church, a pub and a manor house, as well as a farm and a shop.

The Marisco Tavern is the first place most visitors call at, and on fine days, when an excursion steamer has arrived, the sloping green opposite the Tavern, and the nearby walled tea garden, are usually dotted with people eating and drinking. The Marisco Cottage, where Felix Gade and his wife lived for many years, has been converted into a single large room, an extension of the bar. Its walls are hung with lifebelts, each bearing the name of a wrecked ship: *Carmina Filomena*, Genoa; *Amstelstroom*, Amsterdam; *Maria Kariakides*, Andros; *Taxiarchis*, Greece, and many others.

Weddings are rare on Lundy, in the nature of things; it is therefore surprising to find what seems to be a wedding reception going on, with a bride in white and her groom and the male guests in morning suits. In fact, the couple were married on the mainland but have come to Lundy for a ceremony of blessing in the church of St. Helena, and to spend their honeymoon. A chartered helicopter brought the guests across, and will later take them back to the mainland.

Not every building of the village is of stone; there are, for instance, some barns and the double line of timber dwellings known as the Quarters. Yet everything else — house walls and field walls, ancient castle, Victorian church and the Old Light — is built of the island's own substance, granite.

Granite: an igneous rock. Not the oldest, or the hardest, of the earth's rocks, but very old, very hard, strongly grained because it is made up of crystals of quartz, feldspar and mica. It may be of several colours — blue, reddish-brown, green or pink, as well as many shades of grey. It come from magmas, great over-boiled porridge mixtures of molten minerals plopping with gases, found deep in the cauldron of the earth. Off the heat, mineral porridge cooled and set, sometimes in the shape of an inverted pot called a batholith. Infinitely slow cooling produced fine crystals all of roughly the same size, and so the finest granites are those that cooled slowest, giving a pepper-and-salt effect. Evidently Lundy granite cooled comparatively quickly; it is mostly coarse-grained. It has a magnificence that commands attention; its big, contrasting crystals sparkle and seem to alter in the sun. It is a constant reminder of the ancient life of this planet; it makes every modern thing look puny, trivial, evanescent.

The rain has stopped; cloud-cover breaks now and then to let shafts of sun light up the island. On the church porch gates bows of pink ribbon and white beads have been hung, and inside are flowers and more ribbons. The newly married couple, their guests and an archdeacon who presumably conducted the service of blessing have signed the book on the table by the door.

The plainness of the interior is emphasized by its lining of red brick, which the bands of blue (now virtually black) and cream brick do not relieve. Was it cheaper and easier to bring tons of brick and cement from the mainland than to cut and use granite? The inside of the church would surely have been more attractive if it had been built entirely of the island's own stone.

The materials came from many places: stone roof-tiles from Tetbury in Gloucestershire, stone pillars from Purbeck, encaustic tiles for the floor of the chancel and sanctuary from the borders of Wales. On either side of the chancel arch, high up, is a roundel, one bearing the symbol for alpha, the other for omega. A stained glass window commemorates the Rev. Heaven's parents. Outside in the porch is a white marble tablet, unveiled in 1923 by the Bishop of Crediton; the inscription reads:

'In loving memory of
Hudson Grosett Heaven,
Priest, Lord of the Manor of Lundy,
who died in 1916, having accomplished
the dream of his life by erecting this
church to the glory of God.'

Seven of the eight bells that once hung in the tower stand in the porch; their bearings rusted many years ago. One bell was rehung, however, to celebrate the Silver Jubilee of Queen Elizabeth II. A board records that on Wednesday, August 23rd, 1905, eight members of the Gloucester and Bristol Diocesan Association of Change

Ringers, at the kind invitation of the Rev. Heaven, 'rang a true and complete peal of Steadman Triples. This is the first peal rung on these bells'. Crews of ships in the offing on that August day must have marvelled to hear the bells ring out from the usually silent tower.

Below the clock set into the face of the tower is engraved the Latin tag, *Tempus sator aeternitis*, Time is the sower of Eternity. Below it, Harry Hems' statue of St. Helena, holding the cross that is her symbol, gazes seawards.

A few hundred yards to the south-east is the castle. Well restored, its keep converted to three holiday cottages, this oldest surviving structure on the island is hardly recognizable as the romantic ruin that appears as an illustration to Grose's late 18th century ANTIQUITIES.

A path runs down the hill below the house that was once Lloyds' signal station. There, in the 1890s, the submarine cable from Hartland ended, and Frederick Allday kept the island's post office until in 1909 the Admiralty took over the signal station and erected a new building on Tibbett's Hill to house it. Allday moved the post office to the cable house on the outer wall of the castle, today restored as another holiday letting. A little way down the path stands the bungalow known as Hanmers, after a family who often stayed there in the 1930s. It was built for £150, in 1902, by a fisherman, George Thomas and called, with some irony, no doubt, the Palace.

In the landing bay the *Oldenburg* has been joined by the *Balmoral* on an afternoon cruise from Ilfracombe. Both will be sailing in an hour or two. But I'm one of the lucky ones: I have somewhere to stay on Lundy.

Westwards from the castle a track runs past Benjamin's Chair and the site of the kistvaen found in William Heaven's time to the Rocket Pond, at the foot of a long field that occupies the southwest corner of the island, sloping gradually up to Beacon Hill. From the earliest time of the coming of Christianity to the islands of Britain, this seems to have been a priestly place. Halfway up the slope was, until some time around the middle of the 19th century, an enclosure known as the Friar's Garden. A late Victorian writer says that 'when the father of the present proprietor came into possession, this piece of land was enclosed by an old fence in the shape of a coffin . . . Greatly to Mr. Heaven's annoyance, the fence, during his absence on the mainland, was removed, and the Friar's Garden thrown into the ploughland adjoining'.[1] Perhaps the tenant farmer had only been waiting for the chance to plough up the old garden when his landlord's back was turned.

A short distance beyond this point, maps mark Parson's Well, said to have dried up by 1925 and been covered with a slab of stone. Finally, in a granite-walled enclosure, is the site of the ancient chapel of St. Elen, a Celtic saint, and the place where the early Christian memorial stones were found. Excavations of cist burials made in 1969 by Professor Charles Thomas, in co-operation with the Lundy Field Society, are already overgrown with long grass, and bracken rises here and there around the sides of the enclosure. This is one of the most ancient of known burial grounds in Britain; some fifteen hundred years separate the oldest and the most recent burials.

Nineteenth and twentieth century graves occupy the western side, with one or two indecipherable headstones propped against the wall. Here lies William Hudson Heaven, his white marble cross proclaiming him, even in death, as 'Owner and Lord of the manor of this island'. (At the back of the plinth has been added 'Walter Charles Hudson Heaven. Born November 1865. Died 16th October 1929. Elder grandson of W. H. H. Owner of Lundy, 1916-1918'.) A granite cross commemorates William Heaven's eldest son as not only 'Lord of the Manor of Lundy' from 1883 to 1916 but curate-in-charge, 1864-1886 (the last date evidently a mistake) and vicar, 1896-1911. A more elaborate Celtic style cross marks the grave of William Heaven's daughter Amelia 'who fell asleep joying in the peace of God' in 1905 aged 72 years. It was the digging of her grave that brought to light the Tigernus stone.

The graves of Martin Coles Harman, 'Owner of Lundy' and his wife Amy are here, and the ashes of their younger son Albion are marked by a small square granite structure inscribed simply 'Albion Pennington Harman, 23rd June, 1968'.

A big uncut granite boulder lies near the west wall 'In memory of Felix Gade, M.C., known as "Giant". Agent on Lundy 1926-1971. Died on Lundy 28th October 1978 aged 89 years'. The ashes of his wife are buried a few feet away; a tablet records that she was 'Edith Irene Gade. Born September 11th 1895 died August 17th 1973. Known as "Cheerful". She lived for 41 years on Lundy'.

This is not a haunted place. It recalls the tranquil final sentence of WUTHERING HEIGHTS when, after the death of Heathcliff, Mr. Lockwood visits the graveyard and muses that it would be difficult 'to imagine unquiet slumbers for the sleepers in that quiet earth'.

I am to stay in what is known as Old Light East, a small granite-walled building once the lighthouse keeper's store. It has been converted into what is in effect a bed. sit., with its own shower and washroom opposite the entrance. Its simple comforts seem almost luxurious when compared with the bareness of life in the Old Light hostel in the early 1970s.

There are windows on three sides: the largest looks northwards across Ackland's Moor and the old airfield. For an instant, I seem to be catapulted back to the 1930s. Near the Quarter Wall, on the far eastern side of the Airfield, is a monoplane that might almost, at a quick glance, be the Short Scion that Robert Boyd sometimes flew from the Barnstaple Aerodrome to Lundy in the early days of the North Devon Flying Club. Later in the afternoon it takes off, jolting over the rough turf. The pilot somehow pulls the machine into the air before he reaches the cliff edge, banks in a rising turn and flies away towards the coast of Devon. It turns out that his aircraft is in fact an Islander; he has been on Lundy because plans are being discussed to inaugurate a direct air service from Swansea, and even to revive the old link with Chivenor.

It was on Ackland's Moor, named after the Mr. Ackland who leased the island from the Rev. Heaven in the 1890s, that a nine-hole golf course was laid out in 1927 in the mistaken belief that it would bring many golfers from the mainland to stay in the hotel. No trace of greens, fairways and bunkers can be seen now; the big field is open grazing land.

The light begins to fade, and renewed rain squalls spatter the windows. It is time to switch on the light; no need to rely on oil pressure lamps as in the old days. Hardly a hundred yards away the three red-tipped blades of the aerogenerator installed in 1984 turn steadily in the strong wind. On an island where the air is seldom still, it provides a more or less unceasing source of power.

Lights shine out from other windows; people are staying in the old lighthouse keepers' house now divided into two flats, in another former outbuilding within the compound, and in Stoneyhurst, the house just beyond the burial ground which was apparently built for visiting Trinity House inspectors.

Before midnight a full gale is roaring across the island. The Old Light must surely have had a use on nights like this — not least as a beacon to guide sailing ships to the shelter of Lundy Roads.

It's no night for camping, yet down in the village, in a little sheltered paddock beside the Quarters, about a dozen tents, most of them very small, had been erected by late afternoon. What is it like to be lying under a thin skin of proofed nylon in this lashing storm? Or have the tents all whirled away towards Hartland? Perhaps the campers — most of them fairly young — feel that the adventure of Lundy can only be truly experienced by those who endure hardship. I am simply grateful for the reassurance of granite walls.

Chapter Fifteen

Early morning. A cloudy sky, no rain, only a moderate wind blowing. No one to be seen, and no animals, not even a sheep; the island might have been deserted overnight. The track runs north across Ackland's Moor. Just before the Quarter Wall a path slopes down a steep, walled zigzag. I am the first person to come this way this morning: the sticky tension lines of the beautifully-spun webs of some sort of orb-web spider stretch across the path at intervals.

Down and down until one comes to steps, and down again to the roofless ruin of a pair of semi-detached cottages, their shared brick chimneystack remarkably undamaged. A second flight of steps plunges down to the firing platform, with a small building, still roofed: the explosives store. On either side is an old cannon.

It was not until 1863 that Trinity House, in an effort to compensate for the deficiencies of their lighthouse on Beacon Hill, decided to build this fog-warning station, as it was then known, though it later acquired the name of the Battery. Originally the guns were fired at ten-minute intervals; later gun-cotton rockets were used. The national census of 1861 shows that the gunners living here in that year were John Blackmore, with his wife and six children, and Thomas Lee, with a wife and three children. Lee was that Captain Tom, son of William Heaven's tenant farmer, who acted as guide to Philip Gosse and his companions during their stay on Lundy in 1852.

In the 1881 census the gunners are given as John Morgan and his wife, with an adopted daughter whose occupation is entered as 'dressmaker, milliner', and James Thomas and his wife, with no children. A splendid photograph dated 1860 shows two gunners in their Trinity House uniform standing outside the cottages. Their wives are seated; one holds a baby. Possibly these are the Thomases, and the Morgans with their adopted daughter.

As long as a spell of fog lasted, the gunners would of course have been busy loading and firing their old guns, or setting off rockets, but one may wonder how their families — the small children especially — endured the noise. Hardly the conditions for trying to lull a fractious baby to sleep.

All stores — both food and the necessary explosives — must have been brought down the path, but water was available close by. A few yards from the top of the upper steps is a very small weed-choked pond dammed by stones and fed by a trickle from the hillside; the two isolated families must have used this supply.

Did the Morgan's adopted daughter make clothes, and hats, for the ladies of the Heaven family? The latter are said to have visited the Battery quite often. They must have been confident riders on bold and sure-footed ponies; they would ride down the path and one at least is said to have leapt down the flight of steps to the cottages.[1]

Beyond the Quarter Wall the track runs past Dead Cow Point to the area known as the Earthquake. There was a tradition on the island in the 19th century that its series of deep clefts were caused by the great Lisbon earthquake of 1755. (The tradition must therefore have originated in Benson's time, or not long afterwards,) The Victorian geologist Townsend Hall, presenting a paper at the same meeting of the Devonshire Association at which Chanter read his history of Lundy, suggested that 'the fissures on Lundy might be attributed to some still greater disturbance in prehistoric times, and that the subsequent earthquake of 1755 caused a further displacement of the rock masses already loosened and ready to fall'. (Chanter quotes some paragraphs from Hall's paper in his revised monograph of 1877 without acknowledgment.)

Prosaically, modern geologists merely observe that the granite in this place 'is characterised by joints which trend between NW and NNE and dip westerly at 60 degrees or more. This inclination has resulted in much slipping of the granite . . . the granite cliffs above

Dead Cow Point, in the area known as the Earthquake, are deeply cleft by steep joints trending slightly E of N, roughly parallel to the coastline . . . Medium to coarse-grained biotite granite and biotite-muscovite-granite at the northern end of the Earthquake is cut by vertical N-S joints which have dictated massive collapse; huge blocks of granite have slipped and tilted seawards leaving deep N-S clefts up to 30 metres deep'.[2]

Hall pointed out that the fissures are wide enough 'to allow of a person creeping through them, and by descending the natural steps formed by larger blocks which, meeting with some obstacle, have been arrested in their descent, and to see, in the still greater depths beneath the earth, the continuation of those effects which have been left so clearly expressed upon its surface'.

One can certainly scramble down and along the widest cleft without much difficulty. In places the granite here has a pinkish tinge. On turfy ledges grow the little blue flowers of sheepsbit scabious. There's a feeling that a new and final rock-fall might happen at any moment; I find it a relief to climb back into the warmth of the sunshine that is beginning to sweep across the island, and look down into Jenny's Cove, named after a ship that sank there in 1797. She was bound home from Africa with a cargo that included ivory and gold dust. The ivory was recovered, but not the gold dust; said to have been packed in leather bags which rotted, it sank down to mingle with the silt of the sea-bed.

Not long ago, when an east wind made it too hazardous for the *Oldenburg* to put passengers ashore on the landing beach, she sailed round to land some people here, among them an undaunted man of 94, who was helped to clamber up the rock called for obvious reasons the Pyramid.[3]

All along these western cliffs weathering of the granite produced so many vertical and horizontal cracks that in some places the stacks give the impression of having been piled up rather than split naturally. Just north of the Halfway Wall a granite platform shows traces of masonry. The Ordnance map marks this as the site of William de Marisco's mangonel battery, set up in 1222. Possibly he saw Jenny's Cove as a dangerous backdoor to his stronghold.

Around the centre of the island, midway between the Quarter Wall and the Halfway Wall, is Pondsbury, formed by damming a little rivulet that runs down Punchbowl Valley to empty into Jenny's Cove. Paddling among its four islets are half a dozen mallard; they swim shorewards, seeming to hope that the appearance of a human being might mean food. The gleaming water is a mirror for clouds; dozens of swallows and house martins wheel and swoop over it, sometimes dipping down to take an insect just over the surface. Other birds flit in and out of hiding among the wind-stunted bracken. Most look like meadow pipits, a few are wheatears; others I do not know. One undoubtedly misses a good deal by coming to Lundy able to recognize only the more common land, sea and water birds, since the island offers so much, especially when migrants are on passage in spring and autumn.

The name Punchbowl Valley existed at least as early as 1776, as Grose mentions it. The Punchbowl itself has been broken more than once since Philip Gosse described it as 'a basin of solid granite, four feet in diameter and one in depth, of a uniform thickness of six inches'. He thought it might have been the font of a vanished chapel. More recent theories have suggested its use as a mineral washing pan or an abandoned example of the work of millstone cutters. A number of millstones have been found on Lundy; their makers may have exported such stones to the mainland at a date as yet unknown.[4] Loyd refers to the Punchbowl as having vanished, or been destroyed. At some time it was certainly broken into three pieces, and Felix Gade describes going out with Martin Harman one day in 1948 with a bag of cement, a trowel and a bucket and making 'a very reasonable job' of joining the pieces together.

Beyond Pondsbury sheep are grazing, and a few of the island's cattle. On misty days it is easy to mistake boulders for sheep, or sheep for boulders, but today the air is bright; away to the east the line of the Devon coast, from Bull Point to Hartland, stands out. Binoculars show up the long sandy beaches of Woolacombe and Croyde Bay, Saunton and Westward Ho! The sea is the colour to which it gives it name, aquamarine; clouds throw huge shifting patches across it. From the far coast this island must show clearly — but as what? Lundy plain, sign of rain, or Lundy high, sign of dry?

From the broad track running out to the North Light a path leads down to the old quarries. At the entrance to one are the ashes of big fires of rhododendron branches; groups of volunteers have worked on this side of the island in recent years, trying to prevent any further spread of thickets of *rhododendron ponticum* — originally planted in Millcombe by the Heaven family — that overrun these slopes. This is the V.C. quarry, but it would be easy to pass without noticing John Harman's memorial; it is half-obscured by a straggling willow tree that may be at least twenty years old. Behind the tree, a huge inclined slab of granite bears the stone slab on which, within a design of tall palm trees, the young soldier's death and the award to him of the Victoria Cross are recorded.

The path is the bed of a railway line along which trucks of quarried granite were once pulled to the head of a steep incline to the sea; on the beach a jetty was constructed at which the company's ship, the *Vanderbyl*, could come alongside to load. The track ended at a terrace built up to form a tiny marshalling yard for the trucks; stables were built for the draught horses.

Against the rock wall at the back of this terrace is a Heligoland trap belonging to the Lundy Field Society, to be operated by accredited bird ringers; at the moment it is evidently not being used. Southwards, the slippery undulating path leads to Hangman's Hill. At dawn and dusk, in the rhododendron thickets on either side, patient naturalists sometimes watch for the understandably shy Sika deer, survivors of successive cullings. Soon the rut will begin, and stags may gather to fight for precedence on the seaward slope of Tibbett's Hill.

Another path runs up to Quarry Pond, which Martin Harman once stocked with golden orfe. Beside it is the small stone building that was the office of the quarry company's timekeeper. It has become a shelter for walkers; benches line the inner walls, and above another bench outside, in the round space once filled by the timekeeper's clock, a plaque reads:

>'In grateful memory of Felix Gade
>1890-1926-1978'

Higher up the slope are the Quarter Wall cottages. In the 1920s they were still roofed: a photograph reproduced in an issue of the 'Illustrated Lundy News' shows the southernmost cottage with a group of young men who seem to have been staying there sitting outside it. In 1926, Felix Gade, newly appointed as Martin Harman's agent, visited the cottages and found that 'there were no floorboards and the staircases were gone except in the cottage at the south end, so I mounted the stairs and found the roof to be intact except for a few slates on the west side'. Now grass grows where the floors were; no stairs or roofs remain; only the sturdy granite walls stand. Perhaps one day rebuilding will be possible.

Another roofless ruin nearby was the quarry company's hospital. Between this and the Quarter Wall is an area of smooth turf. A group of animals is grazing there: ponies. Lundy ponies, some of them the once-familiar mealy-dun colour. For the second time in twenty-four hours time seems to turn back: these might belong to the herd I saw nearly twenty years ago. I stare at them in astonished delight. Four mares, a stallion and two foals: evidence that the breeding programme begun a few years ago is succeeding. Why should animals of a common species, introduced here less than seventy years ago, seem to represent the spirit of the island? There is little reason in it. Many first-time visitors would probably pass them with hardly a glance; just a few ponies, grazing . . . For all that, the joy remains.

The building that looks most out of place on Lundy is a high black barn standing where the road that has wound its way up from the landing beach runs into the village past the church. However, it is a reminder that Lundy is a working farm, as well as a holiday place. Although a medieval Welsh poet called it Caer Sidi, the Fairy Fortress, other Welshmen called it, matter of factly, Iniswyre, Island of Hay. This suggests that large quantities of winter fodder were regularly gathered to feed a fair number of stock, and things are no different today. It looks as though this summer's hay crop was a good one. Halfway up what is called, with or without irony, the High Street, is a big linhay, re-roofed in recent years, which houses many rolls of hay, as well as farm machinery; more hay rolls, wrapped in black polythene, may be seen out near the Quarter Wall.

In the 1930s the village seems to have resembled the sort of almost self-sufficient manorial farmstead to be found all over England from early times. It had its own kitchen gardens, blacksmith's forge and slaughterhouse; the big stone barn, now converted to a hostel-type holiday letting, had a dozen uses. There were stables, a shippon yard, a meal store and fowl yard. On the western side lay two small fields, Pig's Paradise and Bull's Paradise; despite the whimsical names, they had a practical use.

There was a small brewhouse, which may have dated from the days when the island blacksmith used to brew beer for the Tavern during Mr. Ackland's tenancy; the daughter of the long-serving postman, Frederick Allday, recalled that as a child she used to hear people say how good it was.[5] It was re-used briefly in about 1930, when Martin Harman bought a second-hand brewing plant and Felix Gade and one of the men working on the island produced a quantity of rather cloudy but potent beer; even habitual beer drinkers were apt to fall asleep after more than one pint. It was decided that brewing took up too much time and used too much water — often in short supply on Lundy in dry weather. The equipment was gradually adapted to other purposes.[6]

The most recent attempt to establish a regular brewery on Lundy began in 1984, when an islander named John Ogilvie introduced new plant and began to produce 72 gallons a week for sale in the Marisco Tavern. His sudden death a few years later sadly ended this undertaking.

If the rough track leading through the village is the High Street, its continuation, beyond the five-barred gate at the north end, is the main road. Built by Trinity House to serve the North Light, it runs the length of the island. Beyond the Quarter Wall, at intervals of about sixty feet, great blocks of rough cut granite, each said to weigh more than two tons, act as marker stones. The road was designed for horse-drawn carts; now its traffic is tractors or a Land Rover. Lundy has never known cars or tarmac; its road metal has always been stone. In places it is slightly surprising to find it surfaced with slaty shingle; this was brought up to fill potholes when the new road from the Landing Beach to the Cove was cut.

After a wet summer, every depression in the granite is full of water; a few holes the width of the road still form large puddles.

This morning the ponies are not far from where I saw them yesterday. One mare is resting in the position that in heraldry is called couchant. The foals are on their feet; one suckles his dam as I draw near as though for reassurance. The stallion stands a little apart, confident but watchful.

Beyond the Halfway Wall lies the area called Middle Park, with Tibbett's Hill rising to the east of the track. In 1909 the Admiralty chose this hill, the second highest point on the island, as the site for a lookout. It has become the most northerly of all the island's holiday lettings. An old photograph shows it surrounded by a fence, but it is now encircled by a handsome granite wall.

Two men are repairing a large gap in the Threequarter Wall; this is part of the Landmark Trust's programme of restoration. Just south of the gate leading to the North End is the site of one of the structures Chanter referred to as Round Towers; it has been suggested that it was in fact the base of a windmill. Much archaeological work has been done on this part of the island, as well as at the southern end. In a seventeen-acre plot known as the Widow's Tenement the site of a medieval longhouse and farm has been revealed, lying over a much older Celtic farm system. It is here that partly finished millstones have been found, and the little quarries from which the granite was taken.[7]

For me, and perhaps for many lovers of the island, the wild, remote North End, with its granite outcrops, is quintessential Lundy. Brown Soay sheep and the remnant of the island's herd of feral goats manage to survive on the grazing, but the soil is very thin. In

Benson's time it suffered a fire that burned for days; there have been other fires since. Heather grows on what appears to be bare granite, and bracken is tall on the eastern slopes. In some places big clumps of thrift are dotted with seedheads, though a few still carry one or two pink flowers. On the marshy slopes of Gannet's Combe grow a variety of water-loving plants such as bog pimpernel and bog thistle, marsh St. John's Wort and jointed rush. Offshore lies Gannet's Rock, reported in 1274 to be worth five shillings. By 1321 its value had risen to more than sixty-shillings, and the tenant who kept watch on the gannets 'during the whole season of their breeding' was quit of his rent of two shillings a year.

Gannets have gone from Lundy; to see them as they may have appeared in medieval times one has to go to other islands, such as Grassholm. The puffin too, chosen as Lundy's emblem when the island's first stamps were issued, seemed at one time almost to have vanished. Just before the Second World War there were said to be about 3,500 breeding pairs. Richard Perry, who made this estimate, flew with his wife to Lundy, from Barnstaple Aerodrome, in March, 1939. 'Our dwelling for five months to come was a ruinous cot in the lee of the old lighthouse . . . With its crumbling discoloured walls and bare floors, its leaking roof, smoking chimney and icy draughts, the cottage was less habitable than any shepherd's cot in the Western Isles'.

Perry spent day after day out on the cliffs at this end of the island, watching breeding seabirds; and some nights also, listening to Manx Shearwaters calling as they flew in from the sea, and receiving answering calls from birds in burrows below ground. He studied puffins, kittiwakes, razorbills and guillemots, devoting a section of a book to each. He was a naturalist with the eye of a painter; in his chapters 'The Dancers', 'Burrow Antics' and 'The Fishers' he wrote with unequalled vividness and exactitude of the puffins he was able to observe so closely, sitting by a boulder near nesting burrows, that he might have stretched out his hand to touch them. He recorded that 'the puffin was to make a stronger appeal to me and leave a deeper impression on my mind than any other bird, excepting, for different reasons, the remarkable guillemot'. Although he thought that there might be as many as 10,000 pairs of guillemots and 10,500 pairs of razorbills, the title he chose for the book he published in 1940 was LUNDY, ISLE OF PUFFINS.

When members of a bird club from Exeter University visited the island in 1981 they counted a mere hundred birds, and in June, 1989, the largest number seen in a single day was sixty. Although various theories, including oil pollution, have been put forward for the decline, nothing definite seems to be known.[8]

The once populous Puffin Slope lies to the east of the road, beyond the site of the small building referred to by Grose as a watch house, but later known as John o' Groats' house. It was good, on late summer days on earlier visits, to watch seals from here as they swam around the rocks or hauled out to bask in the sun. Sometimes they would sing, sounding like elderly contraltos trying to get the hang of some half-forgotten tune. There are no seals on the rocks today, but a dark shape moving just below the surface of the water some way from shore turns out, through binoculars, to be a seal swimming northwards.

Where the road ends, steps begin. It's said that there are about 190 in all, but it doesn't seem worth checking. The last and steepest flight has a stout handrail of white-painted iron piping.

The lighthouse, unmanned since 1971, stands sugar-white in the sun. A notice on its unbarred entrance warns members of the public not to intrude. A short length of railway leads from the gateway to the head of yet more steps, zigzagging down to a small quay at which stores used to be landed from Trinity House's own ship, hauled up somehow and loaded on to a truck to be trundled down to the lighthouse.

A second notice warns of the danger of going up this track. On a bank nearby stand two oval-headed stones, both inscribed 'T.H. 1931'. They give no hint of the event they commemorate, but it might be when work to instal an automatic radio beacon was finally completed.[9]

A few kittiwakes appear, flying along the cliffs, but they are silent; there is nothing to recall the great springtime clamour of nesting birds. The whole headland lies in an absolute quiet; even the sea is hushed, waves sluicing gently along the foot of the cliffs.

The Devon coast is less clear than it was yesterday. A trawler is sailing towards Bull Point, probably making for Ilfracombe; otherwise the whole of Barnstaple Bay is surprisingly empty of shipping. It must have been much the same a few months ago, when a speedboat, its engine out of action, was drifting towards this point.

The boat had left Pendine Sands on a Saturday in late June. Aboard were the owner, Simon Roberts, aged 19, Gareth Smith, aged 18, and Steven Evans, aged 15. The engine failed some distance out into Carmarthen Bay, and would not restart. Simon Roberts decided to swim ashore to get help. It was later learned that he lost his life in the attempt. His friends, at first expecting rescue, stayed in the boat as it drifted south across the mouth of the Bristol Channel. They had no emergency equipment and seemingly no provisions. The weather was hot, and for the next two days, lacking shelter, the two boys suffered from sunburn and, presumably, hunger and thirst. They must have been able to see this lighthouse for much of the second day, and known that if they could not reach it, they had little chance of survival. After forty-eight hours in an open boat, without food or water, to swim any distance would have made demands on the stamina of even a fit athlete, yet, somehow avoiding the North Race, Gareth Smith reached the rocks and climbed up to the lighthouse. He probably did not know until then that it was unmanned. He managed to break in, found a telephone and called his own home. His mother alerted the rescue services, and a helicopter from RAF Chivenor flew direct to the North End. Having picked up Gareth, the crew also lifted Steven from the disabled speedboat. Both were taken to the North Devon District Hospital where, with the resilience of youth, they both soon recovered.

Since this lighthouse was first commissioned nearly a hundred years ago, its light has almost certainly saved the lives of many sailors, especially in storm or fog. That it should act as a daymark and refuge as it did on that summer day is surely unique. Although he was helped by daylight and fine weather, it was the resolution and endurance of Gareth Smith that enabled him to make a landfall on this remote, often savage headland, and save both his own life and that of his companion.

In the past few days the wind has been falling from gale to light breeze; this morning the air is still. It is a surprise to wake and see the blades of the aerogenerator standing motionless. The mainland is still visible, but has grown fainter. Around mid-morning a dark dot appears off the hazy snout of Bull Point, moving across a sea like pale blue silk; it resolves itself into the *Oldenburg*, and soon after one o'clock the first passengers reach the village. As usual, the Marisco Tavern is busy. Some people take their food or drinks to tables in the Tea Garden. A seat just inside the garden entrance bears a small metal plaque, inscribed:

"Where summer long we knew the paradise
That only the young and proud may know."
Wendy Anne Mitchell. Poet, aged 21, who died on Lundy, 9th July, 1952'

Felix Gade's description of Wendy Mitchell's accidental death in a fall on the west side of the island, not far from the Threequarter Wall, stands as a sharp reminder of the dangers of going too near the edge of the steep sidelands. There is a particular sadness in the claim made by her poem: if she had lived, she might have come to know that Lundy can offer its paradisal aspect to those much older than she was when she wrote it.

Saturday: changeover day in holiday places. Pale patches of grass show where tents have gone from the campers' field. Outside the big granite barn, hostellers are piling up bulging rucksacks to be taken down to the Landing Beach.

One last afternoon to go — where? Out to the Quarter Wall for one more sight of the ponies, and so down past the Quarry Pond to the quarry terrace and back along the rhododendron path. Where the thickets end it is surprising to see clumps of tall ragwort being allowed to flourish: the plant that can be a slow cumulative poison to grazing stock. A good deal of tree planting has been carried out on the slopes here in recent years: brown plastic tubes protect saplings of sessile oak, ash, birch and alder.

Reaching Hangman's Hill I climb to the Ugly, and sit looking seawards, as members of the Heaven family must often have done. Barnstaple Bay might be a calm lake, and the *Oldenburg* sits on the clear water like a toy boat on a park pond.

There is still time to wander back towards the village. On impulse, I take a narrow path running between tall hedges towards St. Helen's field. A visitor who has been staying on the island is standing by the gate at the end. He and his wife are evidently keen birdwatchers; I've met them several times walking across the island, and he has always been carrying a telescope tripod. He signals me to stop, and points to a small yellowish bird flitting in and out of a gorse bush. A yellowhammer? It flies down on to the path; clearly not a yellowhammer. We watch it for a minute or two; then it flicks out of sight among the gorse.

The birdwatcher comes quietly down the path and says 'I must fetch my wife. She's got the camera'. I ask if he knows what the bird is, but he shakes his head. 'I've never seen anything like it.'

If he is as knowledgable as he seems to be, this is impressive. He hurries away and is soon back; he has been unable to find his wife, but has been joined by another birdwatching visitor. The bird has reappeared, and they spend some time discussing it in low voices.

People are beginning to pass on their way to the Landing Beach. It is time to go. Perhaps the bird is a rarity, of the sort that is recorded now and then in the Lundy Field Society's annual reports: Red-eyed Vireo, Grey-cheeked Thrush, Rose-breasted Grosbeak, Olive-backed Pipit, Veerey. Perhaps, in a day or two, dozens of twitchers will arrive on the island, hung around with high-powered binoculars, telescopes and cameras, and local newspapers will carry some more or less facetious account of the sighting. Perhaps, after all, it isn't anything particularly rare. Possibly I shall never know.

It doesn't matter. It was a pleasure to see it: to know its name is not especially important. It is satisfactory that it should remain a small mystery to take away from this most enigmatic of islands.

NOTES

Chapter One
1. Grahame Farr, WEST COUNTRY PASSENGER STEAMERS. T. Stephenson and Sons, Ltd., Prescot, 1957.
2. A.E. Blackwell, 'Some Critical Notes on the Bibliography of Lundy', Devonshire Association, Transactions Vol. 89, (Exeter), 1957.
3. P.T. Etherton and Vernon Barlow, TEMPESTUOUS ISLE, Lutterworth Press, 1950.

Chapter Two
1. K.S. Gardner, LUNDY, An Archaeological Field Guide. Landmark Trust, no date.
2. Aileen Fox, SOUTH WEST ENGLAND, Thames and Hudson, 1964.
3. K.S. Gardner, op. cit.
4. Gower, Mawer and Stenton, PLACE NAMES OF DEVON, C.U.P. 1931.

Chapter Three
1. This chapter is based largely on 'Henry Clement and the Pirates of Lundy' by P.M. Powicke. 'History', Vol.25, June 1940-March 1941.
2. Matthew Paris.
3. Cal. Patent Rolls, 1232-47.
4. Powicke, op. cit.
5. Rot. Lib. 26, Henry III, m.5.
6. K.S. Gardner, op. cit.
7. G. S. Steinman, 'Some Account of the Island of Lundy'. COLLECTANEA TOPOGRAPHICA ET GENAEOLOGICA, Vol. 4, John Bowyer Nichols & Son, 1837. An edition of 1000 copies was published privately by Martin Coles Harman.
8. Inq. 15 Ed. II, No. 49.
9. A.E. Blackwell, 'Lundy's Ecclesiastical History', Devonshire Association, Transactions Vol. 92 (South Molton, 1960).
10. A.E. Blackwell, ibid.
11. DEVON FEET OF FINES. Devon and Cornwall Record Society, 1939. Nos. 1242, 1255 and 1259.

Chapter Four
1. Steinman, op. cit.
2. A.F. Rowse, SIR RICHARD GRENVILLE, Jonathan Cape, 1937.
3. J.E. Boggis, A HISTORY OF THE DIOCESE OF EXETER. Exeter, 1922.
4. M.M. Oppenheim, MARITIME HISTORY OF DEVON, University of Exeter, 1968.

5. J.R. Chanter, 'Journal of Philip Wyatt, SKETCHES OF A LITERARY HISTORY OF BARNSTAPLE. Barnstaple, 1886.
6. Chanter and Wainwright, REPRINT OF THE BARNSTAPLE RECORDS, London, 1900.
7. Ibid.
8. William Laird Clowes, A HISTORY OF THE NAVY, Vol II. Sampson Lowe Marston and Co., 1897.
9. Cal. S.P. Dom. James I, 1603-10, liii, 100; John Thomas, 'A History of Lundy, 1390 to 1775', Devonshire Association, Transactions Vol. 110 (Tavistock, 1978).
10. Clowes, op. cit.
11. Cal. S.P. Dom. Charles I, Vol V, 55 and 81.
12. Ditto, Vol. CLXIX, 67.
13. Ditto. Vol. CCXXI, 52.
14. Ditto. Vol. CCXXIII, 5.
15. Ditto. Vol. CCXLI, 3.
16. Ditto. Vol. CCXLIV, 68.
17. Ditto. Vol. CCXLV, 20.
18. Thomas Westcote, VIEW OF DEVONSHIRE, London 1845.
19. Tristram Risdon, SURVEY OF THE COUNTY OF DEVON, London, 1811.
20. Thomas, op. cit.
21. HMC Marquis of Salisbury, VI, 35.
22. Acts of the Privy Council XXV, 237.
23. Ibid. 380.
24. K.S. Gardner, op. cit.
25. R. Granville, A HISTORY OF THE GRANVILLE FAMILY, 1895.

Chapter Five
1. John Prince, WORTHIES OF DEVON, Plymouth, 1810.
2. Thomas, op. cit; Cal. S.P. Dom, 1598-1601 Vol. CCLXXIV, 20.
3. Margaret Irwin, THAT GREAT LUCIFER, Chatto and Windus, 1960
4. DICTIONARY OF NATIONAL BIOGRAPHY; and see THE SUPERLATIVE PRODIGALL: A Life of Thomas Bushell by J. W. Gough, University of Bristol, 1932.
5. John Aubrey, BRIEF LIVES, Oxford, 1898.
6. J.W. Gough, op. cit.
7. John Aubrey, op. cit.
8. Thomas, op. cit.
9. Dorothy Osborne, LETTERS TO SIR WILLIAM TEMPLE, Ed. E. A. Parry, London, 1903.
10. Celia Fiennes, THROUGH ENGLAND ON A SIDE SADDLE. Ed. Mrs. Griffiths. London, 1888.

Chapter Six
1. Clowes, op. cit. Vol. I.
2. Cal. S.P. Dom, Charles II, Vol. VII, 146, 155, 177.
3. Ibid, 174.
4. Thomas, op. cit.
5. W.E. Minchinton,'Politics in the Port of Bristol in the 18th Century'. Bristol, 1963
6. For a full account of Benson's activities see THE NIGHTINGALE SCANDAL by Stanley Thomas, Bideford, 1959.
7. 'The Gentleman's Magazine', 1775, p. 447.
8. Ditto 1822, Vol I, p. 283; Thomas, op. cit.

Chapter Seven
1. A.E. Blackwell, 'Lundy's Ecclesiastical History'. op. cit.
2. Francis Grose, THE ANTIQUITIES OF ENGLAND AND WALES, Vol. IV, London, 1776.
3. Lewis R.W. Loyd, LUNDY, Its History and Natural History. Longmans Green, 1925.
4. N. Pevsner, THE BUILDINGS OF ENGLAND: North Devon. Penguin Books, (second edition, 1989).

Chapter Eight
1. For much of the information concerning the Heaven family in this and subsequent chapters I am indebted to the following: Myrtle Langham, 'The Heaven Family of Lundy, 1836-1916', Transactions of the Devonshire Association Vol. 118, 1986; Myrtle Langham, 'William Hudson Heaven', 'Illustrated Lundy News' Vol. 2 No. 5.
2. The inscription may be read in a photograph of Mr. Gade standing beside the marker stone which is in the possession of Knights Photographers, Barnstaple.
3. Felix Gade, MY LIFE ON LUNDY, privately printed, 1978, p. 374.
4. Crockfords Clerical Directory, 1905.
5. Charles Kingsley, 'North Devon: A Prose Idyl', MISCELLANIES, London, 1860.
6. The small son would in time become Sir Edmund Gosse, biographer, linguist and critic and author of that remarkable depiction of the Victorian generation gap, FATHER AND SON.
7. The passage was explored by members of the Shepton Mallet Caving Club in May, 1968, who reported in the Lundy Field Society's annual report for that year that they had found it to be 740 feet long.
8. K.S. Gardner, op. cit.

Chapter Nine
1. John Roberts Chanter, A HISTORY OF LUNDY ISLAND, Exeter, 1877.
2. Quoted in 'The Heaven Family of Lundy'.
3. Michael Bouquet, 'Lundy Granite "Boom"', 'Western Morning News', 3.9.63
4. J.L.W. Page, THE COASTS OF DEVON AND LUNDY ISLAND, London, 1895.
5. J. Gribble, MEMORIALS OF BARNSTAPLE, 1830.
6. Grahame Farr, op. cit.
7. 'North Devon Journal', 28th July, 1870

Chapter Ten
1. Ackland's 'steamer running from Swansea and Ilfracombe' belonged to Pockett's Bristol Channel Steam Packet Co. Contemporary advertisements in the 'Ilfracombe Chronicle' for the 'magnificent sea-going saloon Passenger Steamship *Brighton*' announced marine excursions from Ilfracombe to Clovelly and Lundy at 3s.6d. return for the saloon and 2s.6d. for a fore cabin.
2. Richard Larn, DEVON SHIPWRECKS, David and Charles, 1974, has 2.10 *p.m.*, but this is clearly a slip.
3. His tombstone is inscribed 'Hudson Grosett Heaven, eldest son of William Hudson Heaven and brother of Amelia A. Heaven. Lord of the Manor of Lundy, 1883-1916, Curate-in-Charge, 1864-1886, Vicar 1886-1911. Died February 1916 aged 89'.
4. John Christie, who built the opera house at Glyndebourne, was their grandson.
5. J.L.W. Page, op. cit. and 'Lloyds Weekly Newspaper', 12.11.1911.
6. R.S. Hawker, FOOTPRINTS OF FORMER MEN IN FAR CORNWALL, Appendix F. John Lane, no date.
7. TS in possession of North Devon Athaeum, Barnstaple: no date.
8. 'Hartland Chronicle', 7.6.20.
9. 'North Devon Journal', 17.8.22.
10. 'Hartland Chronicle', 16.7.21.

Chapter Eleven
1. Felix Gade, op. cit. Much of the information concerning Martin Harman and his family, and happenings on Lundy during their ownership, is drawn from this autobiography.
2. For a full account of this case, see Wyndham S. Boundy, BUSHELL AND HARMAN OF LUNDY. Privately printed, 1961.
3. 'Ilfracombe Chronicle', 21.5.48

4. G.M. Bathe and N.J. Scriven, 'The Japanese Sika Deer of Lundy with notes on the now extinct red and fallow population'. Lundy Field Society Annual Report, 1975.

Chapter Thirteen
1. Felix Gade, op. cit., pp. 463-466.
2. 'Western Morning News', 29.3.69.
3. 'Illustrated Lundy News', Vol. 1, No. 1.
4. Gade, op. cit. p.406.
5. Gade, op. cit. p. 487.
6. Gade, op. cit. p. 491.
7. A and M. Langham, LUNDY, BRISTOL CHANNEL. David and Charles, 1970.
8. 'Illustrated Lundy News', Vol. 1, No. 4, P. 9.
9. Elizabeth Parsons, 'Lundy Ponies', Lundy Field Society Annual Report, 1972.

Chapter Fourteen
1. J.L.W. Page, op. cit.
2. L.R.W. Loyd, op. cit.

Chapter Fifteen
1. Myrtle Langham, 'The Heaven Family of Lundy, 1836-1916', Trans. Devonshire Association, Vol. 118, 1986.
2. GEOLOGICAL SURVEY OF GREAT BRITAIN: Geology of Bideford and Lundy Island, HMSO, 1979.
3. Lundy Field Society Annual Report, 1991.
4. K.S. Gardner, op. cit.
5. Mildred Thomas, 'Reminiscences', 'Illustrated Lundy News' Vol. 3 No. 2.
6. Gade, op. cit., pp. 164-167.
7. K.S. Gardner, op. cit.
8. Lundy Field Society Annual Reports, 1981 amd 1989.
9. Gade, op. cit., pp. 103-104.
10. Gade, op. cit., pp. 352-3.

Select bibliography
Boundy, Wyndham S., BUSHELL AND HARMAN OF LUNDY. Privately printed, 1961
Chanter, John Roberts, A HISTORY OF LUNDY ISLAND. Exeter, 1877
Etherton, P.T. and Barlow, Vernon, TEMPESTUOUS ISLE. Lutterworth Press, 1950
Gade, Felix, MY LIFE ON LUNDY. Privately printed, 1978
Gardner, Keith S., LUNDY: An Archaeological Field Guide. Landmark Trust, no date.
Gosse, Philip, SEA AND LAND. James Nisbit, 1865
Gough, J.W., THE SUPERLATIVE PRODIGALL: A Life of Thomas Bushell. University of Bristol, 1932
Langham. A. and M., LUNDY. David and Charles, 1970
Lauder, Rosmary, LUNDY. Badger Books, 1984
Loyd, Lewis R.W., LUNDY, its History and Natural History. Longmans Green, 1925
Page, J. Ll. W., THE COASTS OF DEVON AND LUNDY ISLAND. London, 1895
Perry, Richard, LUNDY, Isle of Puffins. Lindsay Drummond, 1940
Rendell, Joan, LUNDY ISLAND. Bossinney Books, 1979
Steinman, G.S., 'Some Account of the Island of Lundy': COLLECTANEA TOPOGRAPHICA ET GENAEOLOGICA, Vol. IV, John Bowyer Nichol & Son, 1837
Thomas, Stanley, THE NIGHTINGALE SCANDAL. Bideford, 1959
Watt-Smyrk, Joan, LUNDY. Privately printed, 1936

Occasional Publications
Billings DIRECTORY AND GAZETTEER OF DEVON, 1857
'Cave and Lundy Review,' 1824 (continued as 'The North Devon Magazine', 1825)
'Gentleman's Magazine', 1755, 1822, 1889
'Illustrated Lundy News and Landmark Journal', 1970-1975 (15 issues).
Kelly's DIRECTORIES for Devon: 1883, 1889, 1897, 1919, 1926, 1939
'Lundy Chronicle', 1984-1988
Lundy Field Society Annual Reports, 1947-1992
'Lundy Review', 1957-1961 (six issues)
Transactions of the Devonshire Association, vols. 89, 92, 108, 110, 118

INDEX

A
Abbotsham Court, Bideford, 77
Abdul-el-Rehim, Capt., 101
Abonae (Roman port, now Seamills), 8
Ackland, Mr., 77, 84, 127, 135, 145
Ackland's Moor, 89, 94, 127, 129
Adair, Capt., 78-79
Admiralty, 65, 79, 90, 97, 99, 102, 125, 136
Aeolus, 1
Africa, 65, 107, 131
Agdleq, see *Polar Bear,*
Airfield, on Lundy, 93-94, 127
Air Ministry, 102-103
Alexander II, King of Scotland, 13
Alfred, King, 10
Algeria, 26
Allday, Frederick, 84, 85, 125, 135
American Colonies, 43
American Independence, War of, 47
Amstelstroom, 123
Anglia Television, 117
Annery, near Bideford, 23
Annie Vesta, 102
Ansley, 'a malcontent', 32
ANTIQUITIES OF ENGLAND AND WALES, 41, 48, 125
Antrim, Earl of, 109
Appledore, 44, 49, 96, 97, 100, 102
Armada, Spanish, see Spanish Armada
Arundel, 87
Ashton, Winifred, see Clemence Dane
Aston, Adam de, 52
Aubrey, John, 34, 38
Auster aircraft, 103
Australia, 57, 80
Avon, river, 72

B
Bacon, Sir Francis, 33-34
Baggy Point, 2, 30
Bahamas, 108
Baker, Geoffrey, 21
Balaclava, battle of, 81
Balmoral, M.V., 116, 119, 120, 125
Barbellion, W.N.P., 64
Barnstaple, 11, 18, 25, 26, 40, 46, 49, 72, 81, 105, 110
Barnstaple Aerodrome and Flying Club, 93-94, 96, 127, 137
Barnstaple Bay, 6, 7, 103, 114, 139, 141
Barry Island, 72
Barton, Captain, 49, 52

Basset, Sir Robert, 32
Bath, William Bourchier, Earl of, 26
Battery, the, on Lundy, 129-130
Beacon Hill, Lundy, 3, 18, 54, 64, 66, 69, 76, 89, 125, 129
BEAUTIES OF ENGLAND AND WALES, THE, 52
Belfast, 111
Benjamin's Cair, on Lundy, 125
Benson, Thomas, 42-46, 49, 51, 52, 130, 137
Benson Galley, the, 43
Benson's Cave, 44
Berkeley Castle, 21
Bickersteth, Dr., Bishop of Exeter, 75
Bideford, 25, 42, 51, 59, 77, 82, 91, 105, 111, 113, 118, 120
'Bideford Gazette', 73
Billings' DIRECTORY, 1857, 65
Birmingham Mint, 91
Biscayners, 27, 28, 29
Biset, Margaret, 15
Bitte, Walter de, 21
Black Death, 24
Blackmore, John, 129
Blackmore, Robert, 74
Blacksmith's Arms, Bideford, 111
Blackwell, A.E., 6
Blackwood, Sir S.A., 84
Bloody Assizes, 18
Board of Trade, 82
Boggis, Rev. J.E., 24
Bohun, Humphrey de, 19
Boscastle, 113
Botcher, Elmer, 96
Bourchier, William: see Earl of Bath,
Boyd, Robert, 93-94, 127
Bradbury Wilkinson, 90
Bramble Villa, Lundy, 115
Braund, John, character in WESTWARD HO!, 60
Braunton, 32, 96, 122;   Burrows, 122
Brayley, E., 52
Brazen Ward, Lundy, 31, 89
Brian, Sir Guy de, 23
BRIEF LIVES, by John Aubrey, 34, 38
Brighton, P.S., 75, 78
Bristol, 12, 14, 17, 28, 46, 51, 55, 72, 80
Bristol Brabazon, 103
Bristol Channel, 8, 26, 42, 53, 54, 67, 78, 97, 99. 112, 114, 119, 120, 139
Bristol Musem, 69
Bristol Queen, P.S., 99, 118
Bristol Society of Merchants, 42, 54
Bristol Steam Navigation, 72
BRITANNIA, by William Camden, 30
Britannia, P.S., 118

Britannia, Royal Yacht, 111
British Expeditionary Force, 1939, 98
British Museum, 4
Britton and Pickett, 75
Britton, J., 52
Briwere (Brewer) William de, 11
Bronze Age, 7
Brook, Lieut. Oliver, 37
Broughton, 39
Bull Point, 132, 139, 140
Bull's Paradise, on Lundy, 135
Burghal Hideage, 10
Bushell, Anne, 34; Thomas, 33-38, 44, 50
Butler, James, Earl of Ormonde, 23
Butler, Thomas, Earl of Ormonde, 23

C

Caer Sidi, the Fairy Fortress (medieval Welsh name for Lundy, 1, 134
Caldey, island, 28
Calf of Man, 34
Cambria, P.S., 1
Camden, William, 30
Camelford, 39
Camley, near Bristol, 12
Campbell, Peter and Alexander, 1, 118
Campbell Steamers (White Funnel Fleet), 1, 3, 95, 99, 102, 109
Capstone Hill, Ilfracombe, 66
Caracas, 60
Cardiff, 79
Cardiff Queen, P.S., 4, 118
Cardiganshire, 34
Carmarthen Bay, 139
Carmina Filomena, wrecked on Lundy, 123
Cartaret, Lord John, first Earl of Granville, 43
Castle Air Charters, 119
'Cave and Lundy Review, or Critical Revolving Light', 49, 110
Cavern Club, in 19th century Barnstaple, 49
Celtic settlement, on Lundy, 7
Celtic Christian cemeteries, 9, 69
Celtic Christian memorial stones, 9, 126
Celtic Christian missionaries, 8
Central Criminal Court, 93
Chanter, John Roberts, 4, 5, 6, 8, 39, 41, 48, 52, 53, 54, 63, 64, 68, 69, 71, 130, 136
Charge of the Light Brigade, 81
Charles I, 26, 27, 34-36, 38
Charles II, 39
Charlotte, steam packet, 72
Chepstow, 21
Chinchen, Barry, 112
Chivenor, R.A.F. Station, see R.A.F. Chivenor
Chosen Corporation, 92-93

Christie, Augustus Langham, 81, 82, 83, 86, 89, 107
Christie, Augustus Saltren Willett, 81
Christie, John, 145
Christie, William Augustus, 81
Chrymes, Lieut., 49
Churchill, Sir Winston, memorial stamp, 107
Civil Aviation Authority, 119
Civil War, the English. 31, 33, 34-37, 50
Clarendon, first Earl (William Hyde), author of A HISTORY OF THE REBELLION, 35
Clarke, Irene, see Gade, Irene
Cleeve Abbey, Somerset, 52
Clement, Henry, 13, 14, 16, 17
Clerkenwell, 13
Cleveland (Clevland), Agnes, 81; Cornet Archibald, 81; John, 49, 51, 52, 53, 54, 81
Clovelly, 3, 25, 37, 45, 58, 59, 65
Coastal Commnd, R.A.F., 96, 97
Coles, Florence, 87
COLLECTANEA TOPOGRAPHICA, 5
Collins, Charlie, 106
Combe Martin, silver mines at, 35, 38
Comet, steam packet, 72
Constable Rock, on Lundy, 30, 62
Commonwealth Period, 38, 39, 40
Coppinger, Daniel Herbert, 83
Cornwall, county of, 9, 11, 25, 37, 39, 40, 83
Cove, the, on Lundy, 83, 89, 121, 136
Crediton, Bishop of, 85, 109, 124
Cromwell, Oliver, 38,40
Croyde, Croyde Bay, 1, 2, 91, 104, 132
Croydon, 5
Cummings, Bruce Frederick, see Barbellian, W.N.P.
Curragh, 53
Cutcliffe, Rev. Thomas, 49, 51

D

'Daily Telegraph', 93
Dane, Clemence, (Winifred Ashton), 82-83
Danes, 10
Dark, Fred, 82, 89, 97, 114
Dark, Capt. William, 79, 80, 82, 105
Dathan, Lieut., 79-80
Dead Cow Point, Lundy, 130, 131
De Havilland Dragon, 94; De Havilland Rapide, 102
Derbyshire, miners, 35
DESCRIPTION OF DEVON, THE, 32
Despencer, Hugh de, 20, 21, 22
Devil's Limekiln, on Lundy, 3, 64
Devon, 8, 10, 11, 25, 37, 40, 83, 127, 132, 139; Sheriff of, 17, 43
Devonair Ltd., 102-103
Devon Air Travel Ltd., 102
Devonia, launch, 112
Devonia, P.S., 85

Devonport, 78
Devonshire Association, 5, 130; Transactions of, 5
DICTIONARY OF NATIONAL BIOGRAPHY, 10, 33, 39
Dido, H.M.S., 79
Directorships held by Martin Coles Harman, 1932, 92-3
DIRECTORY OF DIRECTORS, 1932, 92
Dixon, Rev., 115
Dodderidge, Richard, 25
Domesday Book, 10
Don Guzman, character in WESTWARD HO! 59-60
Dorset, county of, 24
Drabble, J.E., 102
Drayton, Michael, 6, 109
Drogheda, 14
Dublin, 14, 17
Dugdale, Sir William, (1605-1686), author of MONASTICON ANGLICUM, 21
Duncan, H.M.S., 79
Dunkirk, 99
Dutch Fleet, 40; Dutch Wars, 40, 46
Dyke, John, 103, 106, 109-113, 115
Dynant, Sir Geoffrey, 19

E

Earthquake, the, on Lundy, 4, 66, 130-131
Eastman, Percy, 102
Ecclesiastical Commissioners, 86
Edward I, 19, 20
Edward II, 20, 21, 24
Edward IV, 23
Eliot, Sir John, 31
Elizabeth I, 25, 31
Elizabeth II, 103, 124
Elizabeth, Her Majesty the Queen Mother, 111
English Channel, 26
English Tourist Board, 119
Enston, Oxfordshire, 34, 36
Escott, George, 26, 27
Evans, Steven, 139
Eversley, Hampshire, 58
Exeter, 60, 75; Bishop of, 74
Exeter College, Oxford, 55
Exeter University, Dept. of Zoology, 100; bird club, 138
Exmoor, 6
Exmouth, H.M.S., 79

F

Fairfax, Sir Thomas, 36
Fiennes, Celia, 39; Nathanial, 39; Richard, 36-37; William, first Vicount Saye and Sele, 35-39
First World War, 81, 87
Fitzgerald, Maurice, 13
Flatholm, 72
Fleet, prison, 17
Fogg, Captain, 27

FOOTPRINTS OF FORMER MEN IN FAR CORNWALL, 83
Fort Hill, Barnstaple, 6
Fox, Lady Aileen, 8
France, 18, 32, 33, 43, 46, 97, 98
Franklin, Rear-Admiral, 97, 100
Fremington Quay, 70
Frenchmen's Landing, on Lundy, 42, 89
French pirates, 20, 25, 40-42, 46
Friar's Garden, Lundy, 126
Fulford, Richard, 42

G

Gade, Felix, 56, 87, 89, 97, 101, 102, 104, 109, 113-114, 115, 123, 127, 132, 134, 135, 140;
    Irene, 89, 99, 114, 123, 127
Gannet, Lundy supply boat, 79, 80, 81, 105
Gannet's Combe, 137
Gannet's Rock, 65, 137
Gardner, K.S., 9
'Gentleman's Magazine', 46, 47
Geoffrey of Anjou, 10
Georgeham, 1
George Nott Industries, 118
Germany, 119
Giants' Graves, 68-69
Gibraltar, 76
Gilliat, Col. R.C., 113
Girl Joyce, trawler, 102
Glamorgan, 21, 49, 111
Glen Avon, P.S., 1
Glen Gower, P.S., 99, 118
Glen Usk, P.S. 1, 2, 3, 4, 118
Glenthorne, 82
Gloucester, 8, 17
Gloucester and Bristol Diocesan Association of Change Ringers, 85, 124
Gloucestershire, 33, 75, 124
Glyndebourne, Sussex, 81
Gosse, Philip, 6, 60-67, 68, 70, 76, 97, 112, 120, 129, 132
Gower, Lord (Granville Leveson-Gower, first Marquis of Stafford), 43, 46
Grainger, Ian, 113, 115
GRANITE, play by Clemence Dane, 82-83
Grassholm, 137
Grenville, Sir Bernard, 28, 30, 31, 33
Grenville, Sir Bevil, 31, 34, 35; Grenville, Sir Bevil, Earl of Bath, 35
Grenville, Sir Richard, 23, 24, 30, 33, 43
Grose, Francis, 41, 48, 125, 132, 138
Guiana, 32
Gunstone, Sir Thomas, 44

H

Halfway Wall, 4, 51, 62, 131, 132, 136
Hall, Townsend, 130-131
Hamelin Plantagenet, 10

Hangman's Hill, Lundy, 110, 122, 133, 141
Hanmers, 104, 125
Harman, Albion, 104-107, 122, 126; Amy, 126; John Pennington, V.C., 100, 133; John, 105; Martin Coles, 86-95, 97, 99-101, 103-104, 105, 106, 110, 114, 126, 132, 133, 134, 135
Harman family, 100, 108, 114
Harrow, 55
Hartland, 19, 30, 44, 78, 83, 92, 125, 128, 132
'Hartland Chronicle', 83, 85
Hartland Point, 8, 50, 91, 119
Hartland Quay Hotel, 99
Harvey, Professor L.A., 100, 101, 104
Hawker, Rev. Robert Stephen, 83
Hayward, Sir Jack, 108-110
Heanton Court, 32
Heaven, Amelia Anne, 9, 57, 58, 73, 80, 126; Anne (Cousin Annie), 80; Cecilia, 57, 74; Cecilia Grosett, 56, 57; De Boniot Spencer, 57; Eileen, 112, 115; Rev. Hudson Grosett, 54, 56-57, 61-63, 64, 69, 73-75, 76, 80, 81, 83, 84, 86, 88, 91, 115, 124, 125, 126, 127; John Cookesley, 80; Lucy Sarah, 57, 58; Marion Jane, 57, 74; Marion (Winnie), 57, 74, 80; Walter Charles Hudson, 57, 80-81, 126; William Hudson, 54-56, 60, 61, 66, 68-74, 76, 77, 81, 82, 83, 112, 125, 126, 129; Walter Hope, 57
Hebrides, 7
Heinkel, German aircraft crashed on Lundy, 96
Hemans, Felicia, 66
Hems, H., 75, 125
Henrietta Maria, Queen, 34
Henry II, 11
Henry III, 12-19, 20, 50
Henry VIII, 32
'Henry Clement and the Pirates of Lundy', 11
Hercules, promontory of, 8
Heysman, Donald T., 99
Hill, Charles, 3
Hindon, Betty, 122
Hiscock, Keith, 116
'History of Lundy Island' by J.R. Chanter, 5-6, 69, 130
HISTORY OF THE WORLD, by Sir Walter Raleigh, 41
Hole, Mr., farmer on Lundy, 51, 52
'Home Friend', 61, 62
Honiton, 87
Hunt, Aubrey de Vere, 53, 54; Sir Vere, 53
Huntspill, 14

I

Ilfracombe, 1, 3, 10, 18, 56, 58, 60, 61, 63, 67, 75, 76, 77, 84, 85, 99, 102, 112, 114, 118, 119, 120, 125
'Ilfracombe Chronicle', 75, 84
Ilett, Mr., 106
'Illustrated London News', 110
'Illustrated Lundy News and Landmark Journal', 110-113, 114, 116, 134
Ilminster Grammar School, 56
Incledon, Lewis, 38

Iniswyre, Island of Hay (medieval Welsh name for Lundy), 134
Inkerman, battle of, 81
Instow, 49, 81
Ireland, 8, 16, 27, 28, 29, 53,
Irish Sea, 26
Iron Age, 9
Irwin, George, 102
Isabella of France, 21
Isle of Wight, 34
Italy, 32

J

Jamaica 55, 57
James I, 26, 27, 32-33, 34
Jefferies, Judge, 18
Jenny's Cove, Lundy, 131, 132
John, King, 11, 12
John o'Groats house, 53, 138
Jones, Ruth Pennington (neé Harman), 104, 107
JOURNAL OF A DISAPPOINTED MAN, 64

K

Keast, Diana Kennington (neé Harman) 104, 107
Kelly's DIRECTORY AND GAZETTEER OF DEVONSHIRE, 56, 80
Kennet, H.M.S., 79
Kent, county of, 16

Kent, Duke and Duchess of, 116
Kestrel, fishing trawler, 96
Kingsley, Charles, 58-60, 63
Knapp House, Appledore, 44, 46
Knights Hospitallers, 13
Knights Templars (Order of Poor Knights), 11
Knight Templar Rock, 62, 109
Kohima, battle of, 100

L

Lady Rodney, steamship, 72
Lamitor, Lametry, 30, 89
Lancy, John, 45, 46
Landmark Trust, 109, 111, 113, 114, 116, 117, 118, 119, 121, 136
Lands End, 27, 59
Lane. Rev, Henry Hezekiah. 85-86
Langham, Anthony, 114; Myrtle, 112, 114
Langworthy, Mrs Sarah (neé Heaven), 73, 74
Lansdowne, battle of, 35
Launceston, 39
Lazard Brothers, 87
Lee, John, 60; 64, Robert, 65; Tom, 64, 65, 129
Leigh, Amyas, character in WESTWARD HO! 59-60
Lerina, cutter, 81-82, 89-90, 92, 96, 97, 101, 102, 103, 105, 114
Lewisham, 84
Leyden, Mrs, 98
Lion's Whelps, 17th century naval vessels, 27

Lisbon, earthquake of 1755, 130
Liskeard, 119
Lloyds of London, 79, 84, 92
Lloyds Signal Station, on Lundy, 84, 91, 125
London, 1, 13, 17, 34, 70, 98
'London Gazette', 100
Looker, Maurice, 103
Louis VIII, King of France, 12, 13
Lowestoft, 82
Loyd, L.R.W., 53, 132
LUNDY, by A. & M. Langham, 114
Lundy Band, 83
Lundy Cabbage, 121
Lundy Field Society, 100-101, 102, 103, 105, 116, 122, 126, 133
Lundy Gannet, 105, 112, 118
Lundy Granite Company, 70-71, 73, 82, 94, 100
Lundy Green, 83
'Lundy Island Chronicle', 113
LUNDY: Isle of Puffins, 137-138
Lundy Philatelic Bureau, 90
Lundy Ponies, 88-89, 105, 106, 116, 134, 136
Lundy Postage Stamps, 90, 94, 95, 103, 106-107, 114, 115
Lundy Puffin, 116
Lundy Queen, P.S., 4
'Lundy Review', 111, 112
Lundy roads, 27, 44, 99, 112, 118, 128
Luttrell, Sir John, 23
Lynmouth, 120

M

MABINOGION, THE, 1
Manor House Hotel, 78, 84, 89, 91, 92, 94, 99, 110, 112, 115
Marconi radio telephone installed, 91
Margam, Abbot of, 16
Maria Kariakides, 92, 123
Marine Nature Reserve, Lundy, 116-117
Marisco Castle, 3, 19, 50, 59, 60, 61, 70, 76, 79, 109, 110, 115, 123, 125
Marisco, Lady Agnes, 10; Geoffrey, 12, 13-14; Herbert, 20; John, 20; Sir Jordan, 10, 11; Matilda, 17; Olivia, 20; Stephen, 22; William, son of Geoffrey, 12, 13-18, 45; William, son of Jordan, 11-12, 13, 14, 45, 131
Marisco Cottage, 123
Marisco Tavern and Stores, 3, 4, 89, 91, 95, 98, 101, 109, 110, 111, 114, 123, 135, 140
Marshall, Richard, Earl of Pembroke, 13
Marsland, 82
Martinhoe, 8
Martyn, Rev. Thomas, 48
Maryland, 43
Matravers, John, 54, 55
May, Herbert, 81
Mediterranean, 25, 27
Medway, river, 40
Mesolithic Period, 7
Middlesex, county of, 98

Middle Park, on Lundy, 136
Millcombe House (The Villa), 3, 55, 58, 66, 69, 70-71, 79, 80, 81, 84, 98, 115, 122
Millcombe Valley, 74, 122
Mills, Sir Peter, 108, 109
Minehead, 72
Ministry of Aviation, 94
Ministry of Housing and Local Government, 108
Mitchell, Wendy Anne, 140
Monospar, aircraft belonging to Robert Boyd, 94
Montacute, Elizabeth, 23; William, first Earl of Salisbury, 21, 22, 23
Montagu, H.M.S., 78-80
More, Sir Thomas de la, 21
Morgan, John, 129
Morte Point, 2
Mortimer, Roger, 21
Morwenstow, 83
Mounts Bay, 29
Muller, Rev., 100
MY LIFE ON LUNDY, by Felix Gade, 87, 92-99, 114

N

National Pony Society, 116
National Trust, 75, 108, 109, 110, 113
NATURALIST'S RAMBLES ON THE DEVONSHIRE COAST, 60
Newcastle, 36, 39
Newgate Prison, 17
Newfoundland, 43
Newport, Gwent, 72, 118
New Zealand, 106
Nightingale, ship belonging to Thomas Benson, 44-45
Ninth Whelp, naval vessel, 28
Norfolk, county of, 17
Norman Conquest, 10
Normandy, invasion of, 98, 99
Northam, 29
North Devon Athenaeum, 6
North Devon District Hospital, 139
'North Devon Journal', 5, 77, 78, 82
'North Devon Journal-Herald', 101, 108
'North Devon Magazine', 49
North Light, Lundy, 4, 63, 76, 78, 91, 115, 121, 133, 135, 138-139
Norton, John, 75
Norwood, 5
Nutt, Robert, 28

O

Ogilvie, John, 135
Old Barrow, Roman fortlet, 8
Oldenburg, 119-121, 125, 131, 140, 141
Old Light, 49, 66-67, 91, 92, 97, 100, 104, 105, 109, 116, 123, 127, 128
Old Light East, 127
Ordnance Survey, 76
Orkneyingasaga, 9

Orkneys, 7
Osborne, Dorothy, 38-39
Owen, Lord David, 108
Oxford, 56
Oxford University Genealogical Society, 5

P

P & O Company, 57
Paddle Steamer Preservation Society, 119-120
Page, J. Ll. W., 63
'Pall Mall Gazette', 77
Pamlico Sound, 30
Paris, Matthew, 13, 15-18
Parson's Well, Lundy, 126
Pendine Sands, 139
Pennington, Capt. Sir John, 29
Perry, Richard, 137-138
Pevsner, N., 54
Pig's Paradise, Lundy, 115, 135
Pilton-with-Barnstaple, 10
Piracy, 11-12, 14-16, 20, 25-31, 40-42
Pirates of Lundy, football team, 83
Pisa, 32
Plantagenet line, 11, 32
Planta Genista, (broom), 11
Plumleigh, Captain Richard, 27, 28, 29
Plymouth, Plymouth Sound, 28, 33
Pockett, James, 72, 145
Polar Bear, Lundy supply ship, 118
Pole, Sir William, 32
Pollard, Mark, 29
POLYOLBION, 6
Pomeroy, Major Richard, 37
Popham, Sir John, 32
Pondsbury, 132
Portsmouth, 14
Portugal, 46
Post Office, on Lundy, 77, 84
Powicke, Sir Maurice, 11, 12, 14, 15
Pride of Bridlington, 104
Prince Ivanhoe, P.S., 119, 120
Prince, John, 32
Princess Royal, excursion steamer, 72
Promontory of Hercules, 8
Prudence, Elizabethan ship of Barnstaple, 25
Ptolemy, 8
Puddy, John, 114, Wendy, 113
Puffin Slope, on Lundy, 138
Punchbowl Valley, on Lundy, 4, 66, 132
Purbeck, 124
Pyramid Rock, on Lundy, 131

Q

Quarry Pond, on Lundy, 133, 140
Quarters, the (formerly Paradise Row) on Lundy, 115, 123, 128
Quarter Wall, on Lundy, 3, 74, 94, 127, 129, 130, 132, 134, 135, 140
Queens Own West Kent Regiment, 100

R

R.A.F. Chivenor, 96, 102, 116, 127, 139
Raleigh, Sir Walter, 32-33, 41-42
Rat Island, 2, 30, 110, 120
Ravenswood, P.S., 1
Rendall, George, 29
Reed, Mr., 85
REPRINT OF THE BARNSTAPLE RECORDS, 4
Restoration, of the Monarchy, 39, 40
Ribble, H.M.S., 79
Richard of Cirencester, 8
Risdon, Tristram, 29, 30, 41
Roanoke Island, 30
Roberts, Simon, 139
Rocket Pond, on Lundy, 125
Rolle, Henry, 43
Roman fortlets, 8
Rowse, A.L., 23
Royal Army Ordnance Corps, 110
Royal Greenland Company, 118

S

Sage, Nancy, 84, 85, 89
St. Anne's Chapel, 52
St. Clement Dane, 82
St. Helen's (St. Elen's) Chapel, 21, 24, 30, 39 41, 51, 52, 76, 126
St. Helena, 75, 125
St. Helena's Church, 3, 57, 75, 80, 84, 85, 109, 111, 115, 123-125,
St. James' Church, Ilfracombe, 85
St. James' Fair, 28
St. James, H.M.S., 27
St. John's Valley, Lundy, 122
St. Leger, Sir James, 25; Sir John, 23, 30
St. Sebastian, 27
St. Sidwell's Church, Exeter, 75
St. Trillo, P.S., 4, 109
Salisbury, first Earl of, see Montacute, William
Salkeld (Sakell), Thomas, 26, 56
Salterne, Rose, character in WESTWARD HO! 60
Santa Catharina, Spanish galleon in WESTWARD HO! 59-60
San Tomé, 33
Saunton, 2, 132
Saxons, in Devon, 10
Saye and Sele, William Fiennes, Lord, see Fiennes, William
Scilly, Isles of, 7, 25, 42

Scores, Richard, 42, 43
Scotland, 13, 14, 119
SEA AND LAND, by Philip Gosse, 61-67, 112
Seal Cave, on Lundy, 64
Second World War, 3, 7, 69, 90, 137
Severn, river, 28, 40;   Sea, 29
Seymour, Lord, 25
Shakespeare, William, 400th anniversary memorial stamp, 107
Shetlands, 7
Shirwell Park, 81
Short Scion, aircraft, 94, 127
Shutter Reef, 78
Shutter Rock, on Lundy, 59, 64
Signal Cottages, Lundy, 112
Silures, 8
Skewen, Glamorgan, 111
Smith, Gareth, 139-140
Smith, Sir John, founder of the Landmark Trust, 111, 113, 114
Smith, Rev., 49, 51
Smith, Stanley, 110-111, 112
SOME ACCOUNT OF THE ISLAND OF LUNDY, 5
Somerset, county of, 3, 7, 12, 14, 40, 52, 54, 55;   Sheriff of, 11, 12, 44
Southampton, 27
South Light, Lundy, 2, 76, 78, 91, 110, 115, 121
South Wales, 3, 7, 8, 79, 103
Spain, 26, 43, 46
Spanish Armada, 26, 59-60
Spraecombe Valley, 1
Steadman Triples, 85, 125
Steinman Steinman, G., 5
Stiffe, William, 54, 55
Stone Age, 7
Stoneyhurst, on Lundy, 128
Stukeley,Sir Lewis, 32-33
Surrey, county of, 87
Sutton, Plymouth, 108
Sussex, county of, 108
Swansea, 36, 77, 127
Swatridge, Rev., 84

T

Tapeley (Tapley) Park, 49, 81
Taunton Collegiate School, 56, 57
Taw, river, 10
Tawstock, 26
Taxiarchis, ship wrecked on Lundy, 92, 123
Taylor, George John, 77-78
TEMPESTUOUS ISLE, 6
Temple, Sir William, 38
Tenby, 11
Tetbury, 75, 124
Tettewell, Sir William de, 24

Thames, river, 33
Thames Embankment, 70
Thomas, Professor Charles, 126
Thomas, George, 104, 125
Thomas, James, 129
Thomas, John, 30
Thorpe, Jeremy, 108, 109, 116; Rupert, 116
Threequarter Wall, 4, 31, 136, 140
THROUGH ENGLAND ON A SIDESADDLE, 39
Tibbetts Hill, on Lundy, 125, 133; Tibbetts Point, 92
Tidball, Henry, 74
Tigernus, Tigernus Stone, 9, 126
Torrey Canyon, 107
Torridge constituency, 108
Torridge District Council, 121
Torridge, river, 102
Torrington, 80
Townsend Ferries, 118
Tracy, Henry de, 18, 19
Trefusis, Dr., Bishop of Crediton, 85
Trinity College, Oxford, 56
Trinity House, 2, 53, 54, 56, 66, 73, 76, 84, 100, 107, 128, 129, 130, 135, 138
Tunnicliffe, C.F., 107
Ugly, the (shelter on Hangman's Hill, Lundy), 122, 141
Val, de, 25
Van Os, Herbert, 98
Vanderbyl, Lundy Granite Company's supply ship, 70, 82, 133
Velindra, P.S., 72
Venice, 18
V.C. Quarry, 100, 133
Villa, The, see Millcombe House
Viper, sloop of war, 49
Virginia, 44
Virgin's Spring, 113

W

Waad, Sir William, 34
Wainwright, Thomas, 4
Waldegrave, William, 117
Walerond, Robert de, 19
Wales, 6, 8, 9, 20, 29, 37, 44, 124
Warren, Sir John Borlase, 47-51, 53
Waterloo, battle of, 81
Waverley, P.S., 119
Westall, Wilfred, Bishop of Crediton. 109
Westcote, Thomas, 29, 30
'Western Morning News', 79, 109
Westminster, 13, 21
Westminster Abbey, 38
Westward Ho! 132
WESTWARD HO!, novel by Charles Kingsley, 59-60
Westward Ho! P.S., 109

White Funnel Fleet, 1, 4, 87, 112, 114, 118
Whitley bomber, crashed on Lundy, 96
Widow's Tenement, Lundy, 136
Wilhelmshaven, 120
William I, 10;   III, 41;   IV, 54, 122
William the Marshall, 12, 13
William Williams, 76
Williams, Group Capt. W.R., 121
Williamson, Henry, 122
Woodstock, 14-16
Woolacombe, Woolacombe Bay, 1, 132
Woolfardisworthy, 82
Wormwood Scrubs, 93
WORTHIES OF DEVON, 32
Wright, Dr., F.E., 121
Wright, T.H., 77
WUTHERING HEIGHTS, 127
Wyllington, Sir John de, later Lord Wyllington, 20, 23
Wynkeleghe, Sir Thomas de, 24

Y
York, 22